Southwest Airlines

Recent Titles in
Corporations That Changed the World

Toyota
K. Dennis Chambers

Harley-Davidson Motor Company
Missy Scott

Google
Virginia Scott

Apple, Inc.
Jason D. O'Grady

Starbucks
Marie Bussing-Burks

Southwest Airlines

Chris Lauer

Corporations That Changed the World

GREENWOOD

AN IMPRINT OF ABC-CLIO, LLC
Santa Barbara, California • Denver, Colorado • Oxford, England

Library of Congress Cataloging-in-Publication Data

Lauer, Chris, 1966-
    Southwest Airlines / Chris Lauer.
        p. cm. — (Corporations that changed the world)
    Includes bibliographical references and index.
    ISBN 978-0-313-37863-8 (hbk. : alk. paper) — ISBN 978-0-313-37864-5 (ebook)
1. Southwest Airlines Co. 2. Airlines—United States—Management. I. Title.
    HE9803.S68L38   2010
    387.7'4206573—dc22   2010000934

ISBN: 978-0-313-37863-8
EISBN: 978-0-313-37864-5

14   13   12   11   10   1   2   3   4   5

This book is also available on the World Wide Web as an eBook.
Visit www.abc-clio.com for details.

Greenwood
An Imprint of ABC-CLIO, LLC

ABC-CLIO, LLC
130 Cremona Drive, P.O. Box 1911
Santa Barbara, California 93116-1911

This book is printed on acid-free paper ∞

Manufactured in the United States of America

To Tracy Lee Richmond Lauer and Tovelah Domina Lauer

Contents

Acknowledgments

I would like to start off by thanking the many incredible people who have helped me to complete this book. First and foremost, special thanks go to Greenwood Press senior acquisitions editor Jeff Olson, whose trust in me has made this book possible. Jeff's kind words and professional skills have guided me through every step along the way.

I would also like to thank Chris Murray. As a friend, mentor, and role model, he has helped me time and time again to turn my passions into a thriving career.

In addition, this book would not be possible without the generous help from the many people at Southwest Airlines who helped me discover what a great company looks like on the inside. These wonderful people, who were more than generous with their time, include Brian Lusk, Ginger Hardage, Jon Schubert, David Holmes, Sunny Abercrombie, and Bill Owen. I would like to thank each of them for their time and their enthusiasm.

I would also like to thank the many Southwest passengers who shared their stories with me, including my friends Dr. Daniel Fink, Terry Weiss, Beth M., and Lara Jean Hammond. A heartfelt thank-you also goes out to author and management consultant Charlie Jacobs, who was very generous with his time and expertise.

Two more people who deserve special thanks are Toby Lauer and Tracy Richmond. This book would not be possible without their patience and kindness. Both have sacrificed precious time to allow me to complete this project. I thank them from the bottom of my heart for their encouragement and inspiration.

Finally, I would like to thank Pauline Lauer and Ken Lauer for their endless love and support.

Chapter One

An Introduction to Southwest Airlines

Very few companies elicit as much excitement and loyalty from their customers as Southwest Airlines, the largest low-fare air carrier in the world. When the company's name is mentioned in conversation, those who have flown on the airline perk up and respond with emotional enthusiasm, often saying, "I love Southwest!" or "I only fly Southwest Airlines!" Considering that this company is involved in the business of air travel, a process by which many people are fit snugly into the confines of a long metal tube and hurtled through space at rapid speeds for hours at a time, it's hard to imagine that anyone who has ever experienced the tight space of a crowded airplane and the hustling bustle of an active airport actually enjoys the process. But Southwest Airlines is one of the few airlines that not only makes fans of its customers but even has many of them rave about the company whenever given the opportunity to share their experiences.

The company is famous for a multitude of reasons. Southwest Airlines is the leading low-fare airline in the industry. It has the fastest plane turnarounds of all the airlines and the best on-time record in the industry. Southwest has done this with the lowest employee headcount per number of flights, which helps to save costs. It then passes the savings of its streamlined operations on to its customers.[1]

These attributes help to make the company a success, but they do not tell the whole story of the small upstart that has completely changed the way the airline industry does business.

AMAZED CUSTOMERS

Southwest's customers are amazed and entertained during their flights on the airline by the positive energy of Southwest's employees. Flight attendants at Southwest are famous for cracking jokes, singing to passengers, or simply giving them outstanding customer service during their flights. The airline's pilots are renowned for their in-flight banter, their positive attitudes, and their incredible safety record. No passenger has ever died on a Southwest flight. The company's customer service representatives win awards for their customer-centric behavior, which often goes above and beyond the call of duty. Passengers are also impressed by the fact that, in these days of steadily increasing fees, checking two pieces of luggage is still free at Southwest.

Beyond its remarkable customer loyalty and customer service, Southwest has a worker-friendly human resources strategy that includes wages that are at the top of the airline industry and increased decision making at work for all of its employees. The people who work for the company also enjoy free flights for their extended families, including their spouses, children, and parents.

Southwest is beloved by its customers, employees, and stockholders. As of 2009, the company had turned a profit for all but the first two of the thirty-eight years it had been in business. It is the only airline in history with such an impressive financial record.

AN OUTSTANDING ROLE MODEL

On top of it all, as a result of its success as an airline and a business, Southwest serves as an outstanding role model for companies in all industries, as well as for-profit and nonprofit organizations in all other realms. The employee culture that has been developed throughout Southwest draws accolades and followers every year. Book authors and writers from a multitude of magazines, newspapers, and other publications continually write about Southwest to describe what the company does to create the impressive work and corporate culture that have helped it succeed since the early 1970s.

Representatives of companies from around the world regularly come to Southwest's headquarters at Love Field in Dallas, Texas, to learn how they can apply Southwest's people strategies to their own businesses. Businesses also invite Southwest's leaders into their companies to teach their people how they can create or improve their own corporate cultures. And Southwest gladly shares its techniques and tactics with anyone who wants to learn more, because its leaders and employees simply enjoy changing the world for the better.

A WINNING PROPOSITION

In his book *Leaders Make the Future,* Bob Johansen offers Southwest Airlines as an example of a company that has mastered the ability to offer its customers a "Winning Proposition" that is "both clear and inspirational." In Johansen's view, the Winning Proposition that Southwest offers its customers is "on-time airline performance that rivals the cost of automobile travel, with a touch of fun." Proposing to save people time and money while providing them some enjoyment along the

Southwest Airlines' headquarters is located at Dallas Love Field. (Courtesy Southwest Airlines.)

way is a powerful offer. Johansen adds, "The Winning Proposition provides great flexibility for people to pursue the dream in varied ways."[2]

Today, Southwest employs nearly thirty-five thousand people who serve sixty-eight cities in thirty-five states with more than thirty-two hundred daily departures.

RECOGNITION

Throughout its history, the company has been recognized by a variety of news outlets. In 2007, *Travel Weekly* called the company the "best domestic airline." In 2008, *Fortune* ranked it as a "most admired airline," *SmartTraveler* magazine said it had the "best airfare prices," Time.com called it the "friendliest airline," and the business research and consulting firm Frost & Sullivan said it was the "best overall U.S. airline." With glowing accolades such as these, Southwest Airlines certainly has something to teach other airlines, as well as all other organizations.

The people of Southwest are recognized throughout the business world for their breakthrough corporate culture, which many other companies across the spectrum of industries work hard to emulate. Southwest Airlines employs people in a wide variety of fields, including flight operations, communications, customer service, dispatch, internal auditing, schedule planning, technology, marketing, general counsel, purchasing, safety and environmental, maintenance and engineering, employee relations, facilities, revenue management, and finance. These people show their dedication to the company in numerous ways because the company shows them in a variety of ways that it is dedicated to them. One example of the airline's dedication to its employees is its "Employees Come First" policy. Southwest is one of the only airlines in the world never to have had a mass layoff, even after the airline industry practically shut down after the terrorist attacks of September 11, 2001, and during one of the most difficult economic recessions in U.S. history in 2008 and 2009.

LOW FARES

Most passengers have discovered Southwest Airlines through its reputation for low fares. Few, if any, airlines in the United States or the rest of the world have lower fares. By innovating in myriad ways, the company has been able to save costs and pass those savings along to its customers.

Southwest Airlines cuts costs through value pricing. There are no assigned seats, no meals, no movies, and no first-class travel on its flights. It has the quickest turnaround times in the industry. It is recognized as a quality leader by many studies. It is also honored as a good corporate citizen. *Fortune* magazine calls it a top company to work for.

Many people credit Southwest's superior management and leadership for its many successes throughout its four-decade history. But leaders in the company credit the company's employees for Southwest's success. This type of circular praise—and accolades from across the business and media spectrum—creates a company unlike any on the planet. It is truly a corporation that has changed the world in many fascinating ways.

SUSTAINABILITY

Sustainability is at the heart of Southwest's business strategies. Southwest Airlines separates itself from its competitors and shows other companies how to embrace sustainable business practices that aim to protect the environment in a variety of ways. To guide this strategy, the company has written a Sustainability Vision Statement that it follows to help it make better business decisions. This statement describes Southwest's vision of the future that can be reached through a sustainable business model that balances the company's commitments to its employees, the community, the environment, and its profitability. It goes on to say:

In order to protect the world in which we live for future generations, while meeting our commitments to our Customers,
Employees, and Stakeholders, we will strive to lead our industry in innovative efficiency that conserves natural resources,
maintains a creative and innovative workforce, and gives back
to the communities in which we live and work.[3]

The strategies it embraces while it carries out the business of a
groundbreaking airline include:

- maintaining and promoting a people-friendly company culture
- providing leadership to a constantly changing workforce
- helping the community and charitable programs to get better
  results
- optimizing fuel efficiency, alternative energy options, and
  energy requirements of all ground-based operations
- ensuring suppliers optimize their energy usage and materials
  management
- finding practical solutions to eliminate waste generation
  through source reduction, recycling, and reuse

AWARDS

Here is a list of awards won by Southwest for its sustainable environmental practices:

- U.S. Environmental Protection Agency's Blue Skyways Collabo-
  rative Partner
- President's Environmental Youth Award, U.S. Environmental
  Protection Agency
- Dallas Water Utilities Blue Thumb Silver Award, 2001–2006
- 2007 Port of Portland Aviation Environmental Excellence Award
- 2007 Keep Dallas Beautiful Environmental Excellence Award
- 1995 EPA Region 6 Environmental Excellence Award[4]

These accolades are a clear reminder that Southwest works hard to pre-
serve the environment with its policies and actions. These honors also
demonstrate that the organizations and agencies that monitor and care
about the environment appreciate Southwest's commitment to the planet.

SOUTHWEST'S RECIPE FOR SUCCESS

In 1971, Rollin King and Herb Kelleher had an idea for a new airline that was simple: "If you get your passengers to their destinations

when they want to get there, on time, at the lowest possible fares, and make darn sure they have a good time doing it, people will fly your airline."[5]

Today, their idea has transformed into one of the largest airlines in the United States. As of 2009, Southwest Airlines was flying more than 104 million passengers to sixty-seven cities in thirty-four states. Starting with only four airplanes, the company has grown its fleet to 544 aircraft, all Boeing 737s. Southwest takes great pride in the fact that its fleet is one of the youngest operating in the United States, with the age of its airplanes averaging about nine years.

In 1987, the U.S. Department of Transportation started tracking statistics on customer satisfaction for the airline industry. With its unusual combination of customer-focused policies and customer-friendly corporate culture, Southwest Airlines leads the airline industry with the lowest number of complaints per passenger boarded. This kind of customer satisfaction has led many other companies to copy Southwest's business model and culture in their own industries.

Other innovations that Southwest has pioneered include ticketless travel, lower senior-citizen fares, and a same-day freight delivery service. Southwest.com was also the first airline Web page, and Southwest's blog, *Nuts About Southwest,* was the first corporate blog of its kind for any airline. In addition, Southwest's "Share the Spirit" community programs have demonstrated to all other companies how a business can directly affect the people and communities in the many cities it serves through outreach services and community-building activities.

CREATING VALUE

Beyond the company's industry innovations, "green" practices, customer-friendly policies, employee-first principles, amazing safety record, and financial success, Southwest is a company that creates raving fans because it creates value for all of its stakeholders every day. By separating itself from its competition in a variety of ways, which many have studied but few can repeat with the same kind of success that Southwest Airlines has had year after year for more than thirty-eight years, Southwest has made a name for itself as a corporation that has truly changed the way people travel and the way business is done in the United States and the rest of the world.

Chapter Two

The History of Southwest Airlines: Founders and Leaders

After more than forty-three years as a business in the making, the true stories and myths about the amazing men and women who made it happen continue to be told about Southwest Airlines inside and outside the company. Southwest is no ordinary airline, and it could never have survived and thrived for nearly four decades had it not been for the uniquely talented leaders who imagined a better way to get more people to more of the places they want to go.

ROLLIN KING AND AIR SOUTHWEST

Rollin W. King purchased a charter airline company, the Wild Goose Flying Service, in 1964. Although the company was making very little money—primarily flying passengers on hunting trips to Kerrville, Del Rio, and Laredo, all in Texas—King was determined to keep the company's small, twin-engine Beechcraft planes in the air.

The dream of today's Southwest Airlines began to manifest itself into reality in 1966. While he was talking to his banker, John Parker, King got the idea that would eventually become the modern Southwest Airlines. Parker told King that he was frustrated by the flights that were currently available between Dallas and Houston. He suggested to King that he should fly the planes of his small shuttle company between those two Texas cities. King knew his planes were too small for that type of regular service, but said he'd research the idea, since he was talking to a man who could possibly help him fund such an idea. He also knew that jets would be a better way to fly people between the cities and compete with other airlines such as Braniff and Trans-Texas.

King was a thirty-five-year-old Texas businessman with a Harvard MBA who imagined a better way for people to fly. From his own experiences as a passenger, pilot, and owner of a small air shuttle service, he agreed with Parker that the large airlines of the day—TWA, Eastern, Continental, Delta, and others—were not adequately serving all of the passengers who desired a more convenient and less costly way to cross shorter distances that were too far to drive. He envisioned an airline that would make these trips for lower fares, but his idea was met with skepticism.

THE IDEA

The idea for Air Southwest, which would eventually reincorporate and change its name to Southwest Airlines, was formed around the success of other companies that were already experimenting with a new, no-frills, low-fare model. These companies included Pacific Southwest Airlines (which had no affiliation with Southwest Airlines) and Air California.

Pacific Southwest Airlines, better known by its initials PSA, was started in San Diego in 1949 as an airline that flew to all of the big cities in California, including Los Angeles, San Francisco, and Oakland. PSA was eventually bought by USAir in 1988. Air California, which changed its name to AirCal in the 1980s, served California (and later some bordering states) from 1967 until 1987, when it was acquired by American Airlines. Both of these intrastate airlines were able to undercut their competition in California, such as United and Western Airlines (which was bought by Delta in 1986), with much lower fares because they had lower operational costs thanks to their smaller size, streamlined operations, and lack of interstate routes.

Rollin King wanted Air Southwest to become a similar intrastate airline, flying entirely within the boundaries of Texas and thus bypassing all interstate commerce requirements and the regulations of the Civil Aeronautics Board (CAB) for airlines that flew between states.

While King believed this new idea had vast potential for financial success, the other airlines of the day resisted the concept and the competition. Texas International Airlines, Braniff International Airways, and Continental Airlines challenged King in court. Lawsuits from these major airlines threatened to keep King's idea for a new airline from ever leaving the ground, but King had a persistent attorney with the legal skills and charismatic prowess to battle the large airlines and win. His name was Herb Kelleher.

HERB KELLEHER

Herbert Kelleher was born in Haddon Heights, New Jersey, on March 12, 1931. After graduating from Haddon Heights High School and receiving a bachelor's degree from Wesleyan University, Kelleher went on to receive his law degree from New York University. He later moved to Texas to start a law firm, and there he started working as an attorney for Rollin King.

In 1967, King and Kelleher had a meeting. The two men, both thirty-six years old, discussed the idea of forming an airline called Air Southwest that would serve Texas's three major cities: Dallas, San Antonio, and Houston.

When King told Kelleher his idea for a low-fare, no-frills airline—an airline that had no class system and flew people on trips that were normally handled by bus lines—Kelleher was initially unimpressed, saying, "Well, that's a lousy idea." King replied, "Well, just do it."[1]

And "do it" they did. King told Kelleher to "draw up the papers of incorporation and handle the other legal work for . . . Air Southwest."[2] Those papers created the company that would soon become what we know today as Southwest Airlines.

Debunking the Myths

While the Kevin Freiberg and Jackie Freiberg book *Nuts!* says that Kelleher responded to King by saying, "Rollin, you're crazy. Let's do it."[3] In an interview with *Dallas Morning News* reporter Terry Maxon, King refutes this claim. King explains that Kelleher initially didn't think the idea was a good one: "The fact of the matter was that Herb was trying to talk me out of the airline. He didn't think it was a good idea."

But history shows that Kelleher soon switched his thinking and became a fan of the idea. According to King, "I think time swayed his mind."

Another myth that Maxon debunks in his article is the story of a famous napkin described at length in *Nuts!* As the story goes, when King and Kelleher met to conjure up the idea of Southwest, they drew routes between San Antonio, Houston, and Dallas on a napkin at their table. In Maxon's interview, however, he asked:

> "You guys never drew up a route map on a napkin, though, did you?"
> "No, never did it," Mr. King acknowledged.
> "It is a good story, though?"
> "It's a hell of a story."[4]

Kelleher on Board

With more convincing by King, Kelleher got on board with the idea. Together, the two men created Air Southwest, an airline that would serve the state of Texas.

King got Southwest off the ground by raising millions of dollars and providing some of his own money to incorporate the company. He also paid Kelleher to raise money and fight the legal battles it took to get Southwest the right to fly after the lengthy legal challenges from

Rollin King's Leadership Roles

From the beginning of Southwest's history, Rollin King served as a director and a flight crew member for the company. Eventually he stopped flying to spend more time in his leadership role. King remained on the company's board of directors until 2006, when he retired at Southwest's annual board meeting.

When the company first incorporated, King became the executive vice president, a title he held until 1976. According to *BusinessWeek*, he also served as a member of Southwest's Audit Committee, Executive Committee, and Nominating and Corporate Governance Committee. During this time, he also helped in executive education at the airline's University for People. In addition, he consulted as the principal of Rollin King Associates from January 1, 1989, until his retirement on December 31, 1995.[5]

King retired from Southwest at the age of seventy-six. After forty years with the company, he still owned more than 300,000 shares of the company's stock, which were worth more than $4 million at the time.

Braniff, Continental, and Trans-Texas Airways. King was the largest shareholder in the company when it first incorporated, and Kelleher invested $20,000 of his own money.

EARLY HISTORY

Before Southwest and the California intrastate carriers, most airlines followed federally mandated pricing levels established by the CAB. The new airlines' low fares were unprecedented. With the advent of Air Southwest, which would soon change its name to Southwest Airlines, airline passengers in the state of Texas suddenly had a new way to travel across the vast expanse of the state for drastically reduced fares.

In 1967, Air Southwest was ready to start operations, and by 1968, the company received the authority to fly. But Braniff, Texas International, and Continental did not want to be challenged by a new competitive upstart, so they mounted a tough offensive to keep the airline from ever taking off. The three airlines claimed that the three cities which Southwest proposed to serve already had sufficient air service. They took Southwest to court, trying to keep King and Kelleher grounded.

Four years later, in early June 1971, the fifty-one months of intense litigation in which Kelleher and King fought hard to get the airline

A model of an Air Southwest turboprop aircraft from the early days before South-west Airlines was born. (Courtesy Southwest Airlines.)

started had finally come to an end. Even though the competing airlines had gone to the U.S. Supreme Court to try to stop Southwest from starting operations, the Court rejected their petition. The legal struggles had been settled, and Air Southwest was ready to begin operations on June 18, 1971. But forty-eight hours before the airline had its first flight scheduled, another legal problem was thrown at the feet of the company's founders. Once again, the competitor airlines were trying to stop Southwest from flying to cities they claimed were already properly served by their existing flights.

Only two days remained before Southwest's first flights were to begin. Herb Kelleher had had enough. When the other airlines once again got a Texas judge to stop Southwest from starting its service, he became very angry. He knew there was no basis for the legal challenge to Southwest's ability to fly. As he saw it, "They were simply trying to use their superior economic power to squeeze us dry so we would collapse before we ever got into business. I was bound and determined to show that Southwest Airlines was going to survive and was going into operation."[6] Kelleher challenged the judge and the other airlines because he felt that if Southwest could be kept out of the sky, something was completely wrong with the entire airline system. To him, that meant that something was wrong with the whole structure of society. He could not let the ruling stand.

Kelleher went back to Austin to the Texas Supreme Court. He recalls:

> Before I left Dallas, I told Lamar Muse—who was CEO [chief executive officer] of Southwest Airlines at the time—to go

ahead with our scheduled flight no matter what. Lamar said, "Gee, Herb, what do I do? Suppose the sheriff shows up and tries to prevent the flight?" So I said, "Leave tire tracks on his shirt. We're going, come hell or high water."[7]

The next day, on June 18, 1971, Southwest Airlines kept to its initial schedule and flew its first flight. Kelleher's sheer determination and dogged persistence had paid off for the airline. Demonstrating the power of tenacity and a clear focus on his goals, Kelleher made Rollin King's initial dream of a low-fare, no-frills intrastate carrier in Texas come true.

Love Field

Brian Lusk, Southwest's Manager of Online Relationships and Special Projects, explains that many historical events were taking place behind the scenes before Southwest launched its first flight in 1971. At that time, all of the airlines flying out of Dallas were based at Love Field, the main airport in the region. The Dallas-Fort Worth (DFW) Airport had not been built yet, but in 1968, all of the airlines that would eventually fly out of DFW had signed an agreement to move their operations away from Love Field once the new airport opened for business. Lusk points out, "We weren't an airline then, so we couldn't sign it." This meant that Southwest Airlines was not legally bound to move its operations to DFW.

Lusk adds, "We didn't want to move to DFW because, at the time, it was in the middle of nowhere. There were just farm fields around it. We had the short-haul service to Houston and San Antonio, and we needed the business traffic, which we felt wouldn't follow us over to DFW."

Legal Hurdles

In 1971, after Southwest started flying, the new company started running into local legislation that would force it to move to DFW. Lusk explains, "There was still litigation involved to put us out of operating every time we would receive a new route authority from the Texas Aeronautics Commission, which was the Texas agency responsible for regulating us. We were awarded routes to West Texas and then Texas International [Airlines] would take us to court trying to get injunctions to stop that."

Every time Southwest Airlines tried to advance its business, another legal obstacle in the form of litigation was placed in its way to try to prevent it from moving forward. Still, Southwest persevered.

Eventually, Herb Kelleher's persistence paid off. Lusk explains, "Finally, in 1979, Braniff came out and said, 'We're through fighting

Leadership Teeth

Mukul Pandya, editor and director of Knowledge@Wharton, and Robbie Shell, managing editor of Knowledge@Wharton, honor Southwest's cofounder Herb Kelleher in their book *Lasting Leadership: Lessons from the Twenty-Five Most Influential Business People of Our Times*. Their book describes in detail the most valuable leadership attributes that great modern leaders, such as Kelleher, exhibit in their work.

In the section that describes how great leaders "are able to build a strong corporate culture," the authors profile Kelleher and his ability to change the way businesses work with their people through a more relaxed and comfortable business culture. Writing about Southwest Airlines, Pandya and Shell explain that Kelleher spearheaded Southwest's plan to create a low-fare, no-frills, intrastate airline all the way to the U.S. Supreme Court until its first flight in 1971. But his tenacity did not stop there. They add:

> Later, Kelleher was back in court fighting to keep the airline at Love Field in Dallas. "It was a long and difficult battle. It even continued after Southwest began operations," says Kelleher. "The other carriers exerted a massive effort to get us out of business."
>
> Ultimately, executives at two competing airlines were indicted on antitrust charges.[8]

Pandya and Shell write that these efforts to get Southwest off the ground helped the company earn its wings and build a unique and effective corporate culture "marked by humor, loyalty, and a fierce resistance to corporate bureaucracy."[9]

Two years after Southwest began flying passengers between Houston, Dallas, and San Antonio, its competitors again took legal action against Southwest, trying to get the company to leave Love Field in Dallas. This lawsuit gave Southwest's flight attendants, baggage handlers, and reservations clerks a clear focus that helped them unite together to protect their company. As Kelleher explained:

> Our people were stimulated and challenged and responded with warrior-like spirit. I think that inculcated in them the idea that survival in the airline industry is a game of inches, and by golly, we've got to pitch in. The company became a crusade that they enlisted in. It's been pretty much the same ever since.[10]

Southwest Airlines and the Boeing 727

When Southwest flew one of Braniff's Boeing 727s, it was one of only two times that Southwest Airlines flew a plane that was not a Boeing 737. The other occasion was between 1983 and 1985, at which time Southwest flew six other 727s in California to help it expand into that state when it needed more airplanes to handle the rapidly rising demand there. It leased those airplanes from PeoplExpress Airlines. They were used until Southwest could purchase enough Boeing 737s of its own to replace the leased 727s.

Southwest.' They buried the hatchet and they let us lease an airplane. They let us operate one of their 727s. We operated it for about six or seven months between Dallas and Houston. It was a 'burying the hatchet' kind of agreement."

MARION LAMAR MUSE

The story of Southwest Airlines often hinges on the appeal of legendary men and women. One leader at Southwest who captured the attention of customers and the rest of the business world was the company's first president, Marion Lamar Muse, whose story became a popular Harvard Business School case study that is still studied by management students today.

Muse was a leader of Southwest Airlines who joined the company when it was just an upstart with only three airplanes. In an interview for this book, management expert Charles Jacobs recalls the kind of decisions Muse faced in the early, tough years. Jacobs points to a legendary battle in which Braniff and Texas International Airlines cut their prices below what Southwest could offer. He says this type of predatory pricing was done purposefully to drive Southwest Airlines out of business. The story shows Muse's genius, as Jacobs explains: "So, Lamar Muse doesn't know what to do. He gets up in the morning and he reads the paper and he finds out that they've cut their price to like $13 for a one-way ticket. And he thinks, 'What can I do?' So he goes and he takes out an ad in the newspaper, a double-page ad that says, 'Nobody is going to shoot Southwest Airlines out of the sky for a lousy $13.' And he goes on to say, 'Listen. This is predatory pricing. If you are forced to fly on them because it's going to save you money, we can understand that. But if you fly with us, we'll give you a little present to take home with you.' What they ended up giving were bottles of Chivas Regal Scotch to everybody that ended up flying with them."

Thus, at the beginning of 1973, when Braniff started to offer fares of $13 on the routes flown by Southwest Airlines, Muse offered travelers an option that nobody had ever tried before: he told travelers that they could either pay the full price of a Southwest ticket, which was $26, and receive a free bottle of Chivas Regal, or they could pay the price of $13 that Braniff was offering. In its obituary of Muse, the *Washington Post* noted that "the offer boosted ridership so much that Mr. Muse later credited the Braniff offer for Southwest's financial success."[11]

In Jacobs's opinion, "This was brilliant! What this guy did was, rather than do the logical thing, which means you cut prices and try to survive, this guy did a really counterintuitive thing, and he just brought people's emotions. He told the story of this small upstart and brought people's emotions into play. I think this was just brilliant!"

Muse, like Kelleher, was a master of tapping into the power of a good story to drive people's emotions and attract customers and employees.

Nonetheless, after a lengthy fight with his board of directors over Southwest's plans to expand its services to Chicago, Lamar Muse was forced out of the company. Within three years, he founded another regional carrier called Muse Air, which in turn was bought by Southwest in 1985 after it had trouble competing with Southwest's low ticket prices.

Herb Kelleher once referred to Muse as "a Promethean figure" in the industry and a "cantankerous genius." Kelleher also said of him:

> He was a very aggressive and determined and strong figure, and he got us off to a really good start. He was the perfect

---

Employees Come First

While many other companies claim that "customers come first," Southwest bucks this trend by embracing a different approach. One of the ideas that has helped Southwest build an effective corporate culture is the principle that employees come first. Herb Kelleher founded the company on the idea that happy and productive employees attract happy, paying customers, and his theory has been proven by almost forty years of groundbreaking success.

Kelleher "loves to tell the story of an executive who complained it was easier for a baggage handler to get in to see the chief executive than it was for him. Kelleher told the executive that was because the baggage handler was more important."[12]

By modeling an egalitarian approach to managing employees with his words and approach to leadership, Kelleher has proven himself time and again to be more than a successful leader at Southwest Airlines: He is a role model for all leaders.

---

person—because he was tough, he was competitive, he was hard-minded—to get Southwest Airlines off the ground and turn it into a moneymaker, with all the opposition that we had and as bitter as it was.[13]

Kelleher could appreciate many of Muse's attributes because he exhibited many of them himself during Southwest's legal battles with competitors.

COLLEEN BARRETT

Another key person from the company's early days who continues to have a big voice at Southwest is Colleen Barrett. She was working for Kelleher as his legal secretary in the late 1960s when he was first helping to create and incorporate Southwest Airlines. Barrett was hired by Southwest as corporate secretary in 1978, a position she held until her retirement thirty years later.

While she did not officially join the company until after the company was already in business, the "Original" employees who have been with Southwest since its first days invited her into their ranks. Today, she is an "official" Original.

Barrett was president and director of Southwest Airlines from 2001 until 2008, when she retired. She also served as the company's chief operating officer from 2001 to 2004. During her time with Southwest, she was also the executive vice president of customers and the vice president of administration. Barrett is credited with being instrumental in creating Southwest's famously revered corporate culture. Although she has had many titles during her many years at Southwest Airlines, many of the people with whom she works still call her "Mama" out of loving respect for her nurturing role within the company.

Since retiring from her position as president of Southwest Airlines in July 2008, Barrett has remained active in the company as president emeritus. In that capacity, she serves in an advisory role for all of Southwest's employees and executives. Every day, she continues to help to coordinate the culture teams that she helped to create and many other teams of employees within the organization. (Similarly, even though Herb Kelleher is no longer a board member or CEO, he is still an adviser and chairman emeritus. Southwest's Brian Lusk explains, "Herb is spending a lot of time in Washington [D.C.] helping us there.")

The Golden Rule

One of the underlying principles that has always guided Colleen Barrett during her time as a leader at Southwest is the Golden Rule:

Southwest Airlines president emeritus Colleen Barrett sits in the jet engine of a Boeing 737 featuring Southwest's historic design before it was changed in 2001. (Courtesy Southwest Airlines.)

Treat others as you want to be treated. In July 2008, during an interview at the twelfth annual Wharton Leadership Conference sponsored by Wharton's Center for Leadership and Change and Center for Human Resources, Barrett explained that following the Golden Rule and putting employees first gives them the positive motivation that they carry on to the company's customers: "Our mission statement is posted every three feet, all over every location that we have, so if you're a customer, you've seen it."[14] That mission includes following the Golden Rule.

As president of the company, she said that 85 percent of her time was spent working on employee issues. As a leader who deeply believes in a form of customer service that she calls "proactive customer service to our employees," Barrett puts great faith in the idea that happy and motivated employees are more productive and extend their goodwill to the company's millions of customers each year.

At the Wharton Leadership Conference, Barrett explained:

> When we have employees who have a problem—or have employees who see a passenger having a problem—we adopt them, and we really work hard to try to make something optimistic come out of whatever the situation is, to try to make people feel good whatever the dilemma is that they're dealing with.

This type of family spirit pervades Southwest's culture in a variety of ways, whether this means fashioning a "birthday cake" out of a roll of toilet paper for a traveler on his or her birthday or encouraging employees to bring their children to work with them.

Although she said she is proud of Southwest's healthy bottom line, Barrett said that she also takes great pride in the number of people who have become frequent flyers. These people now number in the millions thanks to Southwest's low fares and unique business model.

Barrett explained that Southwest has done more than bring down the price of flying for travelers. It has also changed the way people travel, and even who those people are. For example, when Southwest began to fly its first passengers out of Love Field in Dallas in 1971, only 13 percent of the American public regularly took airplanes to get to their destinations, and as Barrett pointed out, "Those 13 percent were all male, quite frankly, and they were all businessmen. Women only flew if there was a family crisis. . . . We have changed the way that people thought about flying."

Barrett noted that Southwest's low fares help couples who live far apart from each other stay together. The company also helps divorced parents who live a long distance from their children maintain closer and more frequent contact with the people they love.

An Egalitarian Spirit

During the Wharton Leadership Conference, Barrett explained that she believes that the key to Kelleher's success as the founder and leader of Southwest has been his "egalitarian spirit." She said that Kelleher is the kind of leader who makes employees feel important: "He never embarrassed you—even when you did something really silly or foolish or not too bright. He always supported me and always treated me as a complete equal to him."

With the support of Kelleher, Barrett became Southwest's vice president of administration in 1986. After four years in that position, she was promoted to executive vice president of customers in 1990. Eleven years later, in 2001, she was promoted again, this time becoming the company's president.

As Southwest's president, she was recognized for her exceptional leadership skills, through crises as diverse as the September 11 terrorist attacks and the spikes and drops in fuel prices that followed. In 2007, Barrett won the Outstanding Woman in Aviation Award. Her name has also appeared on *Forbes*'s list of the Most Powerful Women in Business multiple times.

Servant Leadership

The term *servant leadership* first entered the lexicon of leadership theory back in the 1950s when management guru Robert K. Greenleaf started using the term to describe a new way of leading employees to success through compassionate service: You lead best by serving those you lead. Colleen Barrett explains that this is the way she describes her own management style.

Barrett was the earliest proponent of making the Golden Rule part of Southwest's motto and business model. She is also credited with the idea of putting employee satisfaction first, because she saw this as a first step from which passenger satisfaction would naturally flow, creating a profitable business that would then satisfy shareholders.

Southwest Airlines president emeritus Colleen Barrett with four Southwest employees standing atop one of Southwest's Boeing 737s featuring the airline's current design. (Courtesy Southwest Airlines.)

One example of this new business model came during an economic slowdown early in the company's history. Rather than lay off reservations clerks, Barrett encouraged the leaders of Southwest to offer those employees a chance to stay with the company in other jobs.

JIM PARKER

When Herb Kelleher retired from the CEO position at Southwest Airlines in June 2001, the man he appointed to take his place was attorney James F. Parker. Jim Parker became CEO and vice chairman at Southwest Airlines during one of the most difficult economic times to ever strike the company, the airline industry, and the nation: the aftermath of the September 11, 2001, terrorist attacks on the United States.

On that day, the world shuddered as terrorists hijacked four airplanes filled with passengers and flew two of them into the Twin Towers of the World Trade Center and another into the Pentagon in Washington, D.C. Commercial aviation came to a halt that day and for a few days thereafter and then struggled over the next few years to recover from the catastrophe. Many airlines laid off up to 20 percent of their employees to cope with the drop in revenues caused by the attacks, but Southwest refused to lay off its people.

Southwest employee Lusk, who was working at Southwest at the time of those horrific events, recalls, "To me, as an employee, that was a huge event with Southwest. It was probably the scariest time I've ever worked here and also probably the most rewarding time, just the way everyone all pitched in during a really difficult time. I was working in the executive office and I can remember thinking, are we ever going to get our airplanes back up in the air? Because we kept getting different security rules, almost by the hour. It was just a long period of uncertainty."

Lusk and everyone else in the airline business wondered if their industry would survive the calamity. Their jobs were on the line, and they questioned whether their companies would be able to even pay them after the entire airline industry was shut down for several days and the public was hesitant to fly afterward, with its vision of air travel as a safe mode of transportation shaken to the core.

Times at Southwest were tense and worrisome after 9/11. Lusk says that everyone at the company was working so hard to get Southwest's planes back up in the air that "they probably didn't notice until later how perilous a time it was."

Lusk was among the group of people to watch the first airplane leave Love Field in Dallas when the Federal Aviation Administration announced that airlines could resume flights. He recalls, "That was an emotional moment."

General Counsel

Before he became CEO on June 19, 2001, Parker served as Southwest's general counsel starting in 1986. He was also in Kelleher's original law firm in San Antonio before joining Southwest. In an article for *Newsweek*, writer Adam Bryant described their background:

> Jim Parker first met Herb Kelleher in 1977 in a courtroom, representing different parties in a fraud case. They stayed in touch and discovered they had more than the legal profession in common—they both drank Wild Turkey bourbon. Thus began a close working relationship that culminated in March, when Kelleher appointed Parker his successor as CEO at Southwest Airlines.[15]

During each of his three years as vice chairman of Southwest's board of directors and CEO of the company, *Fortune* magazine named Southwest one of the most admired companies in the United States. In 2004, *Institutional Investor* magazine named Parker one of the best CEOs in America.

Although he had helped the company and its family of employees make it through one of their most challenging times after 9/11, Jim Parker did not lead Southwest Airlines for very long. To the surprise of many people at Southwest and the media, Parker retired abruptly on July 14, 2004, after only three years at the helm of Southwest.

What happened? Shortly before his retirement, the message board at *Forbes* was reflecting great dissatisfaction with Parker, who was in the middle of some heated negotiations with the company's flight attendant union that had lasted for more than two years.

Hot Seat

In a *Forbes* article published on March 29, 2004, Aude Lagorce reported that respondents to a poll on *Forbes*'s online message board had given Parker only a 33 percent positive approval. This score was down from the 65 percent approval rating he had received consistently over the previous year.

Along with the drop in popularity among voters in its CEO approval ratings poll, *Forbes*'s readers had more bad news for Parker. Lagorce writes that "the vast majority of the posts direct harsh criticism at Parker, often unfavorably comparing him to predecessor Herb Kelleher, who remains chairman."[16]

One message on the message board read, "All Mr. Parker will ever be remembered for is that he was the little man who destroyed Herb's wonderful airline." Another responder wrote, "He is the beginning of the downfall of Southwest Airlines." And yet another added,

"Everything that Herb Kelleher built has just become a house of cards because of Jim Parker." This type of rising animosity toward Southwest's CEO would soon lead to more than a little bad press.

Three and a half months after the publication of the *Forbes* article, Parker stepped down as CEO and vice chairman of Southwest Airlines. His replacement was Gary Kelly, who had previously been executive vice president and chief financial officer (CFO).

When making the announcement, Southwest's chairman Kelleher said: "Our entire board salutes Jim for his myriad accomplishments and for being an outstanding individual. We will all greatly miss him."[17] The company reported that Parker resigned for personal reasons. Although he would remain a respected business leader while working with other companies, teach courses in frontline leadership and security at MIT, and write a book about his experiences at Southwest, Parker's long tenure with Southwest Airlines was over.

Do the Right Thing

In 2008, Wharton School Publishing published *Do the Right Thing: How Dedicated Employees Create Loyal Customers and Large Profits*, Parker's book about the lessons he learned during his years at Southwest Airlines. In his book, Parker writes that Southwest succeeds because it makes decisions that take its employees' needs into consideration. For example, writing about the days after the 9/11 terrorist attacks, he explains how Southwest did the right thing by putting its employees' needs first. Instead of cutting its workforce by 20 percent like other companies did to cope with the drastic drop in business, Southwest Airlines refused to lay off its people. He points out that the company even went ahead with a $179.8 million profit-sharing payment to employees only three days after the terrorist attacks.

He writes that Southwest was able to do that because it had a conservative financial strategy that left it with enough money to keep its workforce intact. In Parker's words, "Our people built a house of bricks, while others had built theirs of straw. Thirty years of doing things the right way had given us the strength to do the right things during the worst crisis in the history of aviation."[18] Parker got it right himself when he named his book: Doing the right thing is perhaps the primary way Southwest Airlines changed the way companies around the world do business.

Since his retirement from the airline industry, Jim Parker has continued to serve on the board of directors of the Texas Roadhouse restaurant company. He also serves on the Advisory Council for the MIT Sloan Business School Leadership Center.

GARY KELLY

Prior to joining Southwest Airlines in 1986, Parker's successor Gary C. Kelly was a CPA for Arthur Young & Co. in Dallas and a controller for Systems Center, Inc. Like Parker, Kelly is from San Antonio. And like Herb Kelleher, he was born on March 12.

When Kelly was hired by Southwest as the company's controller in June 1986, Southwest had just implemented its new drug-testing requirement for new employees. He was the first person to take a drug test as part of Southwest's hiring process. Three years later, he was promoted to Southwest's CFO position. At the same time, he was also made the company's vice president of finance. In June 2001, he was promoted again to executive vice president. When Parker retired in 2004, Kelly became Southwest Airlines' vice chairman and CEO.

In May 2008, Kelly assumed the role of chairman. In July 2008, he became the company's president when Colleen Barrett retired. Today, Kelly serves as the chairman of the board, president, and CEO for the company. A twenty-two-year Southwest veteran, Kelly has worked closely with Southwest's legendary cofounder, Chairman Emeritus Kelleher and with President Emeritus Barrett to build the nation's fifth largest airline.

Gary Kelly is Southwest Airlines' chief executive officer, president, and chairman of the board. (Courtesy Southwest Airlines.)

Brian Lusk, a Southwest Airlines manager for many years, says that Kelly has done a very good job of carrying on the same type of corporate culture—the "Southwest Way"—that Kelleher originally envisioned for the company. But he also says that Kelly "hasn't been afraid to make changes when we need to make changes." One of those changes that Kelly helped make happen was the shift in the way Southwest assigns the boarding groups in which people enter the plane to choose their seats.

Another important change that Kelly helped to make happen was the repeal of the Wright Amendment, a federal law that greatly restricted how Southwest could schedule its flights and serve its customers. The Wright Amendment would still be in effect had Kelly not spearheaded a definitive battle with the congressional powers that kept the law on the books. Lusk says that this was a natural change that Kelly simply put resources behind to make happen. "It was an evolutionary step," Lusk explains, "when everyone agreed that it was time to do that. He got the ball rolling and Colleen [Barrett] motivated the grassroots effort among employees. And then Herb [Kelleher] really spearheaded the legislative effort in Washington."

Gary Kelly introduced a new boarding procedure that allows passengers to line up at these columns when their seating group is announced. (Courtesy Southwest Airlines.)

REGULATORY ROADBLOCKS

Let's take a closer look at the battle over the Wright Amendment, since it shows yet again the power of persistence in Southwest's business success. In 1978, all of the airlines in the United States were controlled by federal regulations, except for companies such as Southwest Airlines, PSA, and Air California because they flew entirely within the borders of a single state. These few airlines were controlled by state economic regulations.

All other airlines flew under the jurisdiction of the Civil Aeronautics Board. This regulatory organization told all of the national airlines where they could fly, what they could charge, and what they could serve to their passengers. Basically, every aspect of their service was regulated by this federal regulator.

In 1978, mainly due to the success of Southwest, PSA, and Air California, the airline industry was deregulated. At that point, airlines could begin to fly wherever they wanted to fly, charge whatever they wanted, and provide whatever kinds of services they determined that their customers wanted.

Deregulation

Once deregulation took place in 1978, Southwest Airlines wanted to begin flying out of state from Love Field in Dallas. Jim Wright, who was Speaker of the U.S. House of Representatives at the time, was from Fort Worth, Texas, and he wanted Southwest to move its operations to the Dallas-Fort Worth Airport instead of remaining at Love Field. After ten years of litigation, Wright spearheaded the passing of a bill in Congress that restricted service at Love Field so that Southwest could not fly nonstop from Love Field to anywhere outside of Texas except for the four states that border Texas.

The Wright Amendment was put in place by Congress to protect the Dallas-Fort Worth Airport from Southwest's low-fare business model and to ensure that American Airlines and DFW could compete in a changing business environment. Under the Wright Amendment, all airlines were barred from ticketing passengers on flights from Love Field in Dallas to any destination that was not a state on the Texas border. (The amendment did not apply to airplanes with less than fifty-seven seats.)

Over the years that followed, Southwest Airlines learned to live with the restrictions imposed on it by the Wright Amendment. After 1998, the regulation was loosened to allow Southwest to serve Alabama, Mississippi, and Kansas. In the meantime, customers outside of that region continued to request service from Southwest.

After Gary Kelly took over the top spot as CEO at Southwest, the time was right for the airline to address the restrictions of the Wright

Amendment. In 2005 and 2006, Southwest fought hard to get the law repealed by the new Congress that was now in office. But American Airlines and DFW, the site of American's hub, battled Southwest to keep the Wright Amendment intact.

In the middle of that fight against the amendment, St. Louis and Kansas City, Missouri, were opened up to Southwest's flights from Love Field. This slow chipping away at the amendment gave Southwest Airlines greater hope that it could get the entire Wright Amendment overthrown. The prospects of doing this were greater than ever, but it still looked like it would be years until the law could be changed completely.

A Compromise

"In the meantime, there was a move to start a compromise with the city of Dallas, with Fort Worth, and with American, and with us, and the DFW airport," Lusk recalls. "They came up with a local compromise." This compromise, which passed through Congress at the end of 2006, is the law that is still in effect today. Starting in December 2006, Southwest gained the legal right to fly anywhere from Love Field.

As Lusk explains the compromise: "The airplane just has to stop at another point. We'll fly from Love Field to Denver, and the flight will stop at Amarillo, which is on the way. Or we'll fly to Los Angeles and we'll stop in Albuquerque. Or we'll fly to Orlando and we'll stop in New Orleans, and we can sell tickets all the way through. The only thing we can't do until 2014 is fly nonstop to those destinations."

In 2014, the Wright Amendment will completely disappear from the law books, leaving Love Field to operate as if it were any other airport. The only exception is that there is a limit to the number of gates that Southwest Airlines can operate out of Love Field in Dallas.

A PROUD DAY

Here's an indication of the company's success on Gary Kelly's watch: On July 21, 2009, Southwest Airlines released some very good news. After a rough period of earnings for the first part of the year, Kelly posted the second quarter 2009 earning results for the company, which were a surprise for many who had watched as the economy wreaked havoc on the profits of other airlines. Instead of posting a loss, which it had done the prior quarter, Southwest reported to its shareholders that its net income for the second quarter of 2009 was $54 million. In the recessionary economic climate of the second quarter of 2009, the posting was a welcome profit of which the company leaders were very proud.

Highlights of the company's second quarter 2009 announcement included the facts that Southwest Airlines had:

- earned $2.6 billion in total operating revenues
- had a cash flow of $135 million from its operations
- raised $540 million through its financial activities
- been able to repay $400 million it had borrowed in 2008 on its $600 million revolving credit facility

Good News

Each of the above announcements was another piece of good news for the company. In his statement to the press (in Southwest's unique writing style), Gary Kelly, the chairman of the board, president, and CEO of Southwest Airlines, explained that the latest earnings report was an "enormous achievement" for the employees of the airline:

> I am exceptionally proud of them, their Warrior Spirits, and their terrific operational and Customer Service results. We continue to stay focused on weathering this economic storm and managing alarming jet fuel price volatility. Thanks to the superb efforts of our People, we have a tremendous body of work completed, underway, and planned to sustain our financial health by enhancing the Customer Experience and generating substantial new revenue opportunities.[19]

One of the ways Southwest enhanced the ability of customers to interact with the company was by making its Web site, www. southwest.com, even easier to use. Adding wi-fi service to its flights is another initiative the company launched to provide its customers with more options when they fly on the airline.

Southwest versus Continental

While Southwest reported a profit, other airlines continued to struggle. For example, on his blog for DailyFinance, an AOL money and finance site, journalist Douglas Mcintyre reports that Continental Airlines made a much less fortunate announcement on the same day that Southwest posted a profit for the second quarter of 2009. The headline for his story says it all: "Continental Loses $213 Million, Will Cut 1,700 Jobs, Raise Fares." In his story, he notes that "revenue [at Continental Airlines] dropped almost 23 percent to $3.13 billion."[20]

Mcintyre also reported that baggage fees at Continental continued to rise. The first bag a passenger checks in at the airline would now cost $20, $5 more than previously. A second bag would cost $30 for passengers who don't use the airline's online check-in service. More costs for passengers in the form of additional types of fees were also expected at Continental. And Continental Airlines is not alone. Most of the other large carriers were also raising their baggage fees as well.

Meanwhile, Southwest Airlines continues to charge nothing for a passenger's first and second checked piece of baggage. (On June 17, 2009, passengers began to have to pay a charge of $50 each for a third through a ninth bag, and $110 for a tenth and additional bags.)

Now that we've seen how Southwest attained its place in the airline industry, let's look at what makes the company really unique: its culture.

Chapter Three

Southwest's Unique Corporate Culture

The corporate culture at Southwest Airlines has received accolades from all across the globe. Guided by a unique set of people-centric values, the employees and leaders at Southwest continue to follow traditions and principles that combine with their caring attitudes and their focus on their customers to create a corporate culture that has made Southwest Airlines a role model for organizations around the world for more than thirty-eight years.

A CULTURE BORN IN A HOSTILE ENVIRONMENT

During the early days of Southwest's existence, times were tough. The hostile environment the company faced as a result of legal and competitive challenges from other airlines created a survival mode at the company that had a powerful bonding effect among Southwest's first employees. That early culture was based on people helping each other make it through difficult times using humor and hard work. Today, what started as a unique employee culture that was built on surviving daily struggles still continues to be successful and productive.

In those early years, working at Southwest Airlines was often very difficult for its employees. Sometimes they would work without knowing whether they would get paid. Original employees still tell stories about how their family members would join them at work to help them do what needed to be done to keep the business in operation.

"The Warrior Spirit"

Those early days at Southwest were when the long-standing tradition of different work groups and departments pitching in to help each other began. Today, this is what is referred to as "the warrior spirit" at Southwest.

In May 2006, the W. P. Carey School at Arizona State University hosted an event that featured a presentation by David Ridley, who had recently retired as vice president of marketing and sales at Southwest after eighteen years with the company. Today, he is back with the company as senior vice president of marketing and revenue management. During his presentation, Ridley described the warrior spirit at Southwest this way: "Warrior spirits have passion—they care, they have emotions. Some organizations and companies are clinics, and that's fine—the Southwest way is not for everyone, but I'd rather work in an organization where people show their emotions—express themselves."

He added that a warrior spirit also has a "servant's heart," reflecting a part of the "Southwest Way" that is often advocated by Southwest's president emeritus Colleen Barrett.

Living the Southwest Way

Of all of the values that Southwest works to keep alive in its people, the one that sets all employees at the company from those at other organizations is "living the Southwest Way." The three major elements of the Southwest Way are:

1. *A warrior spirit.* According to Ridley, this means that people "understand hard work and sweat on the brow."
2. *A servant's heart.* Ridley explains, "People who are other-oriented, not self-important, who put others first—these are the people who will deliver service like Southwest Airlines."
3. *A "fun-LUVing" attitude.* "We take our customers and our competition seriously—not ourselves," says Ridley.[1]

These three dimensions of the Southwest Way help to make the company unique while also enhancing the customer experience. While many of its competitors have worked hard to emulate Southwest's success by lowering their fares and cutting costs, these three elements of Southwest's people-centric strategy are part of the secret ingredient that makes Southwest's employees so productive and the airline so successful.

Positive Values

Southwest manager Brian Lusk says that the Warrior Spirit "is still a predominant trait among our employees; the fact that it is a fight. Everyone is after us. We've had other examples. Not to the degree of those early days, but when United, USAir, Continental, [and] Delta all started low-fare airlines within an airline just to take on Southwest and put it out of business, that was another time where we had to come together and make sure that we were all on the same page and all fighting the same fight."

In a company of thirty-five thousand employees, positive values that incorporate fun, love, hard work, service, and egalitarian principles can have a powerful effect on keeping people working together toward the same goals. Southwest has always been a proponent of putting its people first and treating them fairly. These basic ideas have helped to instill an entrepreneurial spirit of caring and creative cooperation among Southwest's people.

SUNNY ABERCROMBIE AND THE CULTURE SERVICES DEPARTMENT

Sunny Abercrombie is the senior director of culture services at Southwest. She says that describing the corporate culture at Southwest Airlines can be a difficult undertaking because it entails so many different things.

Abercrombie says that the three parts of the Southwest Way—a warrior spirit, a servant's heart, and a fun-LUVing attitude—accurately

Sunny Abercrombie is senior director of culture services at Southwest. (Courtesy Southwest Airlines.)

capture the Southwest culture because "we work hard and we play hard, so that kind of covers the warrior spirit and the fun-loving attitude, but we always strive for good customer service. That falls under the servant's heart. That could also cover the community events that we do and the charities that we're involved with."

The primary recipient of Southwest's charitable giving is the Ronald McDonald House program, which is a major part of the Ronald McDonald Children's Charities. Every year, Southwest sponsors the Southwest Airlines LUV Classic golf tournament and gives the proceeds to many Ronald McDonald Houses around the country. So far, over the past twenty-three years, these proceeds have totaled nearly $11 million.

Culture Services

But the culture at Southwest goes beyond charitable giving. Abercrombie's department, Culture Services, works hard every day to keep the Southwest Way alive among all of the company's employees through a variety of activities.

One of the ways the members of Southwest's Culture Services teams keep the company's groundbreaking employee culture alive is through their support of Southwest's volunteer Culture Committee. Team members also support Southwest's employees in the field and their local culture committees. In addition, they support employees who have "life events" take place, such as the birth of a baby, the death of a family member, or a serious illness in the family.

The Culture Services teams also pass along all praise from customers to Southwest's employees. Every employee who receives positive feedback from a passenger in a letter or e-mail receives a commendation directly from Southwest's CEO Gary Kelly, thanks to the work of the Culture Committee.

Celebrations

Celebrations are extremely important at Southwest, so the Culture Services Department is also in charge of the many corporate events and festivities that take place each year. Abercrombie speaks for herself and her fellow employees when she says, "We're lucky, because we do have leadership that believes you should spend money on [celebrations]. A lot of places, they want to have this great culture, but they don't really want to spend the time or the money to make it what it is. My department does that."

At one point or another, the team members in Southwest's Culture Services Department reach out and touch virtually every one of the more than thirty-five thousand employees on Southwest's payroll.

Colleen Barrett: Once Again the Catalyst

Culture Services is made up of twenty-eight full-time employees. Twenty-three years ago, Sunny Abercrombie was the only person in Southwest's Culture Services Department. Since then, she has seen the department and its duties grow as the company has grown. Abercrombie explains that Colleen Barrett made the department what it is today: "I've worked for her twenty of those twenty-three years."

The many teams that make up Southwest's Culture Services Department have always been a part of Southwest's environment, but they formerly reported to different bosses in different departments. Barrett was the leader who pulled them all together into a consolidated group that focuses on similar responsibilities. "We have the same goals," Abercrombie explains, "so it just makes sense that we all work together."

Internal Customer Care

One of the teams in the Culture Services Department is Internal Customer Care. That's a team of five people whose job it is to acknowledge employees' life events. Through an internal Web site, they stay in contact with administrators out in the field, who input all pertinent information about their people. For example, if a flight attendant has a baby, that person's boss will put all of her information into the company's computer system, including when the baby was born and how long the flight attendant will be on maternity leave. Staff members in Internal Customer Care will then send out a card and a gift for the baby from Southwest. If an employee is sick, Internal Customer Care sends cards and gifts to that person to help him or her recover.

When Abercrombie's husband was recently in the hospital recovering from a major surgical procedure, he received many cards and gifts from Southwest. She says, "It doesn't seem like a lot, but it really is when he's on his back." Abercrombie adds, "You get these cards and you realize there is somebody thinking about you when you're trying to recover." She says that kind of support really makes a difference when a loved one is sick.

Southwest's Culture Services Department receives about 1,500 submissions from managers in the field each week. These submissions include an employee's child graduating from school, an employee being injured on the job or at home, or an employee being out of work for a serious illness. Somebody from Southwest will acknowledge each of these events with an appropriate phone call, card, or gift.

If an employee is out of work because of a serious illness for six months, a year, or more, a Culture Services representative will call that employee regularly to make sure that person is receiving his or her benefits and answer any questions that employee might have regarding finances or any other types of difficulties. If the person from Internal Customer Care cannot help, he or she will put the employee in touch with somebody from Southwest's Benefits Department who can get that person the help he or she needs.

Customer Communications

Another group of employees who work under the Culture Services umbrella is Southwest's Customer Communications Team, which is also called the "Good Letter Team." If a customer either writes a letter or sends an e-mail to Southwest to compliment an employee for a job well done, the message—rather than going to the Customer Relations Department, which handles customer complaints, Rapid Rewards questions, or other types of more technical questions—goes to the Customer Communications Team. The team also receives compliments from fellow employees. It typically gets more than five thousand letters and e-mails each month (since they started to accept letters by e-mail, the Customer Communications Team receives about two thousand more messages every month).

Southwest employs ten people on its Customer Communications Team. Five of them are researchers, and the other five are responders. If the letter is vague and contains only tidbits of information about the employee rather than a full name, it is up to a researcher to identify the "blonde flight attendant on the Wednesday afternoon flight from Philadelphia" who was complimented by a passenger on that flight.

Along with a commendation that goes to the employee, the customer also receives a personal response written by one of the responders on the Customer Communications Team and signed by Southwest CEO Gary Kelly. Administrators in the group are responsible for researching the issue, writing the copy, and distributing these letters to everyone involved in a timely manner.

Culture Activities

The Culture Activities Team is another group of employees that works under the auspices of Southwest's Culture Services Department. This team has been part of Culture Services longer than any of the other teams. It consists of five full-time employees, along with two summer interns who help team members get all of the details right and avoid long nights of work before the big events they manage.

This team is responsible for coordinating all of the Culture Committee's nearly sixty visits that take place throughout Southwest's vast system. These visits entail Culture Committee volunteers going out into the field and helping employees in airports, flight attendant bases, pilot bases, maintenance bases, and Customer Support Centers (once called the "Reservations Department").

During each visit, Culture Activities representatives and Culture Committee volunteers perform service projects that range from grilling burgers for employees working the baggage ramp to arranging a "Pizza Day" for employees in the airport or setting up an ice cream bar for fellow employees on busy travel days. "Whatever it is," Abercrombie explains, "it's just a way to show those employees that we appreciate their hard work." The duties of the Culture Activities employees include coordinating and setting up the events, ordering the food, arranging transportation, and making hotel reservations for the volunteers.

The Culture Committee

Southwest's Culture Committee is composed of more than one hundred volunteer members. These Southwest employees, on their days off, help the Culture Activities representatives execute the visits they coordinate around the many Southwest locations in airports around the United States.

Culture Committee volunteers include people from all levels of Southwest Airlines, from mailroom employees to company officers. The volunteers picked for the Culture Committee are made up of a diverse cross-section of employees. From coast to coast, north to south, Abercrombie strives to make sure different regions and areas of the country are represented on the Culture Committee, as well as all ethnicities and pay scales.

The Culture Committee volunteers meet four times a year for an all-day, mandatory meeting in which Culture Committee officers address hot topics that are pertinent within the company. The volunteers are also encouraged to brainstorm ideas that they think would be helpful in the field, including ways that the Culture Committee can show employees that the company appreciates them. Through these brainstorming sessions, the volunteers bring ideas to the table that might have been missed in previous meetings. During these sessions, volunteers also discuss any employee complaints that they might have heard.

Abercrombie explains that the Culture Committee meetings "go all day, 8 A.M. to 5 P.M. We pick these people because they are the types of employees who truly care about the direction our company is taking. So, they can get quite intense. They don't hold back."

Volunteer Terms

Volunteers on the Culture Committee serve for three years. Their terms are staggered, so about thirty Culture Committee volunteers end their terms each year. These people recommend other employees within the company who might be good candidates to come in and take their places on the Culture Committee.

To vet these nominees, Culture Services employees talk to their supervisors to make sure the recommended volunteers are in good standing with the company and are available for the assignment. Abercrombie points out, "One thing we would never want to do is pull these people away from their jobs if they're at a station that is understaffed, where they really need the people to be there."

Responsibilities of volunteers on the Culture Committee include three visits out into the field each year. Abercrombie says that she is surprised by the number of volunteers that the company gets to work on their days off, because Southwest is 85 percent unionized and there are certain union rules that they have to follow regarding working on their days off. "It is pretty interesting that they want to do it and they keep up with it like they do," she adds. Culture Services has to turn down people who want to be on the Culture Committee all the time because their station is already represented in the group or there are no more current openings.

The Alumni Team

Years ago, volunteers for the Culture Committee were released from service after their three-year commitment ended. But many of them wanted to continue to help their fellow employees even after their time on the committee was over, so Culture Services created what it calls the "Alumni Team." Today, there are more than two hundred members of the Alumni Team. They no longer attend the four annual, mandatory Culture Committee meetings, but they do meet occasionally and are asked to perform two service visits in the field each year. Since these people often still retain the benefit of being able to fly anywhere on Southwest as a standby passenger, their flights to these visits are free.

Because there is no time limit to membership on the Alumni Team, the individuals volunteer as part of it for as long as they want. The enthusiasm of team members is endless. Abercrombie says, "We even have people who leave the company who want to stay on there. We have some retired employees who just show up for those meetings or say, 'I want to go to this visit in Sacramento. I want to go see the employees there, so can you sign me up?'" These people are welcome to join the Culture Committee volunteers. Abercrombie says the Alumni Team members help out tremendously.

Spirit Parties

Another responsibility of the Culture Activities team is putting on what Southwest calls "Spirit Parties." The team puts together two of these each year. These large corporate events are open to any employee in the company, as long as they are off work and can get on a flight to attend. These well-attended events are extremely popular among employees, who treat them like a family reunion at which they can reconnect with coworkers who are often widely dispersed around the country. "We encourage our employees to move around the system, and this is just a great way that they can reconnect," Abercrombie explains.

A recent Spirit Party took place in May 2009. Since the economic climate in the country was pretty bad at the time, members of the Culture Activities team reached out to its vendors to help Southwest keep its costs low. One way they did this was by holding the event in Las Vegas, which not only welcomed the event but also helped to pay for nearly all of it. Rather than hold the event at a glamorous casino, Southwest held its event on Fremont Street in downtown Las Vegas.

The city of Las Vegas donated the venue, a light show, and entertainment. Beer vendors donated beer. Coca-Cola donated soft drinks. Southwest paid for the food. About seven thousand people showed up for the festivities. Abercrombie, who attended the event, says, "It was unbelievable!"

Southwest was able to hold a relatively inexpensive bash while Las Vegas enjoyed a kick to its economy. With all of the money those people funneled through the city's hotels, restaurants, bars, and casinos, Las Vegas made a great return on its donations, and Southwest's employees enjoyed a huge party and great hospitality.

Because of the continuing economic struggles in the United States, Southwest decided to cancel the Spirit Party it had scheduled for September 2009. Abercrombie explains that it seemed a little too soon to go back to Southwest's vendors for more donations, and it also might have sent the wrong message that the company was partying while the rest of the country was struggling through the recession.

Southwest's Annual Awards Banquet

At Southwest's annual awards banquets, the company honors every employee who has served with the company for ten, twenty, twenty-five, thirty, or thirty-five years. Each employee can bring a guest to the black-tie event, which is held in Dallas every year. At this sit-down dinner, Southwest also awards its President's Award. Every year, employees nominate their peers for this award, and winners are chosen by Southwest's Senior Management Committee.

Although Southwest canceled its planned Spirit Party in the fall, the company still put on its annual awards banquet in June 2009. On June 18, fifty-eight employees from a cross-section of the company's many departments received a President's Award. These people were invited, with a guest, to the banquet, where each received a plaque and a bonus check. Three thousand employees attended Southwest's 2009 awards banquet at the Sheraton Hotel in downtown Dallas, which was the only venue in town with a ballroom large enough to hold the event.

Entertainment at the banquet included a comedy routine by *Saturday Night Live* regular Seth Meyers and music by *American Idol* finalist Michael Johns. Southwest's rapping flight attendant David Holmes also entertained the crowd with his rapping skills. Abercrombie explains, "He did a special rap all about what it means to be a President's Award winner and celebrate those years of service. I thought that was really cool. He said he was more nervous doing our show than he was being on Jay Leno. He said, 'I have to see these people again!'"

Other special guests who appeared on stage at Southwest's 2009 awards banquet were the two Southwest flight attendants who competed on the fourteenth season of the CBS reality show *The Amazing Race*: Christie Volkmer and Jodi Wincheski.

Along with the recipients of the awards, their dates, and the employees of the company who joined them, all of Southwest's officers also attended the event. Abercrombie, who worked closely with the five members of the Culture Activities team to coordinate the event, recalls, "It was just a lot of fun and a great night. It takes a tremendous amount of coordination. You have to get all of the right people in the right seats and move the show through. It's a long night, from 6 P.M. until 2 in the morning."

This event and many other regular Southwest events keep the Culture Activities team very busy throughout the year.

"Doing Fun Things"

Other large Southwest annual events include a Chili Cook-off in April, a system-wide Halloween celebration in October, and activities on all of the major holidays, which it celebrates with its employees and customers in a program called "Own the Holidays." For example, in July 2009, two members of the Culture Activities team helped everyone celebrate Independence Day by flying around the country dressed as the Statue of Liberty and Uncle Sam, greeting customers and employees, distributing prizes, and getting their pictures taken with them. Many of these photos were later posted on Southwest's Web log, *Nuts About Southwest* (www.blogsouthwest.com). Abercrombie explains, "We're just always doing fun things to make things fun for our employees and our customers."

The Culture Ambassadors

The fourth team that makes up Southwest's Culture Services Department is called the "Culture Ambassadors." These eight people

In 2005, these are the leaders of Southwest Airlines on Halloween: Gary Kelly (dressed as Captain Jack Sparrow from the film *Pirates of the Caribbean*), Colleen Barrett, and Herb Kelleher (dressed as the legendary fictional defense attorney Perry Mason). (Courtesy Southwest Airlines.)

work primarily with the Culture Activities team. There are culture ambassadors for each of Southwest's "Big Six" work teams: ground employees, flight attendants, cockpit pilots, mechanics, customer support services, and provisioning agents. Five of those work teams have one culture ambassador each, but since there are so many ground employees working for Southwest across the United States, three culture ambassadors represent this work team.

A culture ambassador is a liaison between Southwest's executive office and employees in the field. These ambassadors are always on the road. They check in daily with headquarters to keep in touch with the latest news and information or for support from the people there. Culture ambassadors also help local culture committees, coaching local leaders and ensuring that they have the tools they need to keep their local employee cultures alive and thriving.

LOCAL CULTURE COMMITTEES

While Southwest has a national Culture Committee of a hundred people, the company also supports local culture committees that operate only in their individual home cities. These local committees choose and run their own events and programs for their own people. They establish their own rules, but are supported with money, resources, and people from Southwest's headquarters. The committees are also eligible to receive money from their local budgets, and they raise additional money for themselves through local fundraisers that they conduct for themselves.

People from the Culture Services Department staff help these local culture committees in any way they can. Support from senior management is a vital ingredient in the recipe for the success of the entire culture system at Southwest. Abercrombie says: "The great thing for us is we've always had Colleen Barrett or Herb Kelleher supporting us in all of our culture stuff. Now we have Gary Kelly. Colleen and Herb are still here, but I report to Ginger Hardage. She's our senior vice president of culture and communications. We still have great support from upper management, which, to me, is what it takes. You've got to have it there, or it's not going to work."

Abercrombie says that support from Barrett was vital for the culture at Southwest to take root. Her "servant leadership" philosophy has been integral to creating the renowned corporate culture that continues to flourish within Southwest Airlines. The functional structure of Southwest's Culture Services Department came directly from Barrett, according to Abercrombie: "She lives for providing great customer service. She lives for nurturing people. She is the 'mother' of all of our . . . employees, and she always will be."

THE ORIGINALS

Support from leaders and from past employees keeps the corporate culture of Southwest Airlines healthy and growing. To help current employees learn from the stories from Southwest's history, the Culture Services Department taps into the wealth of knowledge and experience of those who know more about the company than anyone else: the "Originals."

Eleven of the first employees of Southwest Airlines from 1971 are still working at Southwest. Seven of them are the original flight attendants from Southwest's first flights, one is a manager in flight operations, another works as part of Southwest's ground crew, one works as a dispatcher, and the last works in maintenance.

On special occasions, Southwest invites the Originals to come in to Southwest's headquarters and talk about their experiences to current employees. "We always have these people on hand," says Abercrombie, "because the stories they can tell are absolutely amazing." For example, "They'll talk about the time we had to sell an aircraft because we didn't have any money to pay our bills."

When the Originals speak to customers and employees, they describe the struggles of a new airline working hard to get into the air. They also talk about how the company had no money for advertising during its early days, so the flight attendants would go down to the streets of downtown Dallas, Houston, and San Antonio in their uniforms—hot pants and knee-high boots—and hand out flight schedules for the airline's four flights to everyone they met.

Every year, Southwest also conducts what it calls "Rocking Chair Sessions," at which it will bring in some of the Originals, who will sit in rocking chairs in front of an audience of employees and tell their stories from Southwest's bygone days. Topics include how they were hired, the early interview process, and what their uniforms were like in the early days. This type of storytelling keeps the history of Southwest alive, while also linking the company's early corporate culture to the lives of the people who work there today and into the future.

Storytelling is an important part of Southwest's employee culture. Abercrombie says that meeting and sharing stories with the Originals who have been with the company for nearly forty years helps her put her twenty-three-year history with the company into perspective. "I think storytelling can work whether you've been here ten years, twenty

In the company's early years, Southwest's flight attendants wore a uniform featuring hot pants and white, knee-high boots. (Courtesy Southwest Airlines.)

years, or forty years, and sometimes even with new employees talking amongst themselves, just sharing experiences," she adds.

THE UNIVERSITY FOR PEOPLE

One place where stories play an important role in sharing and promoting Southwest's corporate culture is the airline's University for People, which handles all of the company's training. New hires spend time there getting oriented and learning about the company in its "Fly" program. They also receive training on their specific jobs at Southwest during their time at the University for People.

Employees can also volunteer to take more training classes at the University for People. Anyone in a lower- or mid-level management job can apply to become part of Southwest's manager-in-training program.

In an interview with *American Executive* magazine's Jill Rose in 2007, former Southwest CEO James Parker noted with pride, "We could have almost qualified as a higher education institution at Southwest; we did so much training at so many levels."[2] That training has paid off for Southwest in the form of better-educated, upwardly mobile employees; smarter leaders; and a unified workforce that shares similar educational experiences. The University for People helps to put Southwest's employees on the same page.

While Southwest's employees learn how to succeed at Southwest during their training at the University for People, Southwest also spends time learning about its new hires through Myers-Briggs Type Indicator training and other types of personality testing. These tests help employees and leaders understand their strengths and weaknesses in a variety of areas. Other offerings at the University for People include classes on interview techniques, presentation skills, writing and editing, and improving public speaking skills. Many different kinds of computer training are also available.

As a facilitator of the company's culture, Southwest's Sunny Abercrombie has been involved in helping people get the training they need from the University for People for the past eight years. She describes the program: "For any of our up-and-coming leaders, there's a Level One and a Level Two. Level One is for people who are going into management, and Level Two is for people going into higher-level management, whether its senior management leadership or director leadership."

EMPLOYEES COME FIRST

Southwest's employees know they come first and that their leaders have their backs. By hiring people for their attitudes more than their aptitudes, Southwest has created a corporate culture made up of employees who serve their customers with a unique joy that manifests itself in numerous ways. Some flight attendants sing to their passengers. Some tell jokes to flyers as they board the plane. Sometimes they dress in costumes on holidays. It's all about being yourself and celebrating what makes you unique.

They gained "permission" to act in such ways thanks to the company's leadership. Company founder Herb Kelleher, for example, is famous for accentuating his eccentricities, whether it is his reputation as a Wild Turkey–drinking chain smoker or a lover of parties and celebrations. When Kelleher was CEO, he turned his love of Halloween into a tradition at Southwest Airlines. One Halloween, Kelleher showed up dressed as Elvis driving a Harley-Davidson. The entire company still parties on that special day of the year, at its headquarters and at the gates of its airport terminals.

After Kelleher retired as CEO, his successor Gary Kelly demonstrated his belief in and support of carrying on Southwest's audacious corporate culture by dressing up on Halloween as Edna Turnblad, the bouffant-wearing mother from the movie and musical *Hairspray*, complete with pink dress and prosthetic breasts. Other years, Kelly has dressed up as Gene Simmons from the rock band Kiss, Captain Jack

For Halloween in 2007, Southwest Airlines CEO, president, and chairman of the board Gary Kelly dresses as Edna Turnblad from the musical and film *Hairspray*. (Courtesy Southwest Airlines.)

Sparrow from the film *The Pirates of the Caribbean*, and Billy Gibbons from rock band ZZ Top.

By symbolically embracing the corporate culture at Southwest Airlines with costumes, celebrations, and traditions, the current leaders of the company perpetuate the successful culture of Southwest's past into a colorful and exciting future.

Abercrombie sums up her career as a long-term Southwest employee in terms that describe a satisfying work experience in a corporate culture that has changed her life: "It's just a fabulous place to be. This will be the last job I have. When I leave here, it will be because I'm retiring to not work. It's just not that much like work to me. There's a lot to it. There's a lot of hours, but somehow you just get more out of this than knowing that you've come to work and gone home."

Chapter Four

A Role Model for Other Organizations

In business schools around the world, Southwest Airlines has been used as a case study from which students and future leaders can learn about how a business can thrive through a positive corporate culture and successful business practices.

For several decades, business writers and academics alike have embraced Southwest Airlines as a benchmark company that can serve as a role model for any organization in any industry. The *Harvard Business Review* has published several case studies from which top leaders in various industries have learned how to apply Southwest's low-cost model and leadership principles to their own work. Other top business schools, such as the Wharton Business School at the University of Pennsylvania and the Tuck School of Business at Dartmouth College, have also published many stories that describe Southwest as a business from which for-profit businesses and nonprofit organizations can all learn. In addition, the *New York Times*, *Forbes*, *Fortune*, *BusinessWeek*, and many other publications have printed numerous stories that highlight Southwest's powerful business strategies.

JACOBS ON LEADERSHIP

One business consultant and author who studies management and organizational effectiveness is Charles S. Jacobs. In his book *Management Rewired*, Jacobs describes what the latest neuroscience teaches us about the ways people learn to lead. He writes that storytelling is essential to the process of learning about leadership, and that great leaders tell great stories from which their people can gather meaning and make sense of the lessons they need to learn.[1]

The story of Southwest Airlines offers students of business and future leaders many lessons about how a company can succeed by offering its people a storyline that they can wrap their brains around. In a recent interview for this book, Jacobs pointed out that Southwest's story of being a small upstart company trying to survive amid the mounting pressures of larger competitors really resonates in the minds of the company's customers and employees and helps the airline stand out as an underdog worthy of support.

Emotionally Appealing Stories

When combined with the lessons learned from great literature and other types of storytelling, the lessons provided by Southwest Airlines offer all businesses ways to improve how they work. In the same way that great literature touches its readers through emotional stories that deeply connect to their hearts, Jacobs says that the story and idea of a company that puts its people first appeals to the emotions of customers and employees, which creates fierce loyalty.

Capturing the power of a story like Southwest's ties in perfectly with the latest brain science, which shows that people are driven more by their emotions than by anything else, including monetary rewards. Because Southwest has built its personality and corporate culture around many of the factors that resonate within the human brain, Jacobs says that it is no wonder that the company succeeds. He adds that Southwest Airlines is a company from which other companies can learn, even those outside of the airline industry.

"To me, there are a couple of things that are really astonishing about Southwest Airlines," says Jacobs. "Number one, this is a company that has consistently made money in an industry where nobody else makes money."

Management Rewired

Jacobs says that the approach Southwest's leaders have taken to connect with customers and employees also taps into a storyline that resonates with people. He recalls that Herb Kelleher "was legendary for wearing a grass skirt to employee meetings. He really believed that this was all about hyping people up and getting them excited. And then they would figure out what they needed to do, rather than managing their behavior and saying, 'Here's your policy and procedure.' Instead, he managed the mindset and let people come up with their own policies and procedures within a range that worked for the business."

Create Mindsets

Southwest is a great example of many of the points Jacobs makes in his book, including the principle that managers must look to creating mindsets rather than simply expect traditional techniques such as periodic performance reviews to motivate their teams to excellence.

"We must be really cautious what we learn from other companies because there are so many variables at play," Jacobs notes. "I think you can learn [from company case studies], but it's not as simple as what we think it is because situations are so incredibly different."

One of the main points of Jacobs's book is also one of the main things that leaders at Southwest Airlines have done for years: Tap into the human spirit. "It does amazing things for you," Jacobs believes.

Jacobs explains that Southwest has tapped into something powerful. He says that when "you redefine the model of American industry, you begin to leverage what Americans do really well, and it ain't producing Toyotas! That's not our culture."

He explains that leveraging the spirit of freedom to innovate at work using your own personal skills and talents gets people very excited about their work: "They not only get incredibly excited about it, but all the data is telling us that it makes businesses much more successful. We've just got to break away from this feudal mindset that we operate with. The companies that do it, like Southwest, end up being tremendously successful. And the companies that can't—which ones do you want to name, from TWA to Delta—are the ones that fail. Think of the resources that these guys had to compete against Southwest, and they could never get it together. They'd start these great airlines and they inevitably would fail. I think Southwest is a great company."

HERB KELLEHER'S LEADERSHIP PHILOSOPHY

In October 2008, Southwest chairman emeritus Kelleher spoke in front of an audience of business executives, company managers, and other leaders as part of a forum conducted by the leadership development company HSM Global. In his presentation, titled "Building a People-Focused Culture," he described his personal leadership philosophy, which involves putting Southwest's "internal customers"—its employees—first, *before* external customers and shareholders. "The synergy, in our opinion, is simple," he said. "Honor, respect, care for, protect, and reward your employees, regardless of title or position, and in turn, they will treat each other and their external customers in a warm and in a caring, hospitable way. This causes external customers to return, thus bringing joy to shareholders."[2] That joy is reflected in the positive attitude that pervades the company's people, on the ground and in the air.

The leaders at Southwest Airlines don't believe that their job is simply to provide more reliable airline services at lower fares: They also believe that they must add a spiritual element to the mix. This includes increased levels of humanity—more fun, more kindness, more service, and more "servant-leadership," from leaders to employees and from employees to customers. Kelleher explains, "The intangibles of spirit, in our view, are more important than the tangibles of things." By connecting to the aspects of humanity that cannot be measured in numbers and statistics, and by focusing on morality and ethics, Southwest draws passengers to the uniquely warm and fun-loving environments it creates on its aircraft.

Along with a positive environment, "psychic satisfaction is what employees and even external customers are primarily seeking," Kelleher explains. "If anyone doubts the value of esprit de corps, I suggest a talk with the United States Marine Corps. Esprit gets things done, well and fast." Like the Marine Corps, Southwest creates a unity among its people that turns an intangible core of common values and motivated camaraderie into tangible, teamwork-based results.

Being upfront with employees entails constant communication. That's why Kelleher says that leaders must learn how to communicate. But they must learn how to communicate in a language that their people can understand. By avoiding the boring nature of corporate-speak, leaders are better able to reach their people. He also advocates the creation of employee services and "employee care departments" within an organization that stay in touch with people and help them solve their problems. The key to doing this effectively is showing employees that they are valued as individuals and not just as workers. As Kelleher explains: "Through word and by deed, [the company should] join in their every personal exaltation, such as the birth of a baby, and their every personal mishap and grief, such as the death of a relative. You always hear from us when anything important happens in your life."

This type of intimate communication between leaders and employees creates deep connections among the people at Southwest and their peers and leaders. It also improves their morale. It might cost more for a company to put so much attention into these types of personal interactions, but the increased productivity of Southwest's people demonstrates that they appreciate and value this kind of bond with their workplace.

Kelleher says that even though the idea of a company's culture is elusive, "that does not diminish the significance and the power of culture." Southwest's groundbreaking culture continues to flourish even after Kelleher has stepped down as CEO and chairman. Although he is no longer running things, the culture that he helped put in place decades ago has stood the test of time.

EXTRAORDINARY LEADERS

When discussing the difference between leadership approaches, the coauthors of *The Extraordinary Leader*, John H. Zenger and Joseph Folkman, hold up Southwest Airlines as a company that exhibits successful

leadership practices that other organizations can emulate. They compare an elitist approach to leadership with Southwest's more egalitarian approach. They point out that many companies in the past
"focused all their leadership development efforts on a small handful of
people who were currently in senior positions, or who were perceived
as being 'high potential' because of some psychological testing and
interviewing, or assessment center procedures."[3]

Zenger and Folkman believe that Southwest Airlines and the U.S.
Marines are two organizations that stand out in stark contrast to the
old way of determining who within a group deserves to be developed
as a leader. They suggest that Southwest and the Marines "have con-
cluded that the organization will be stronger if everyone is a candidate
for development." They add:

> This approach is especially appealing to those who believe that
> leadership is necessary at all levels of the organization—not just
> at the top. It also appeals to those who believe that many peo-
> ple, not just those who occupy positions of authority or who
> have multiple subordinates, can practice leadership.[4]

By creating a flexible hierarchy that allows people at all levels to
provide their input to the running of the organization, Southwest keeps
its employees and managers motivated and engaged, while also keeping the leaders at the top of the company in touch with innovations
that are apparent only to the people who work directly with customers
on the front lines and their direct supervisors.

BLUE OCEANS

When Southwest Airlines developed a new business model for the
airline business by creating the low-fare category of carriers, the company was simply exploring a new price category in the marketplace
where few had ever ventured before. Several decades later, business
experts W. Chan Kim and Renée Mauborgne put a name to this type of
business strategy. In their best-selling book *Blue Ocean Strategy*, they
compare two types of marketplaces: "red oceans" and "blue oceans."[5]
A *red ocean* is a marketplace where many others compete like sharks,
battling over a shrinking pool of profits. On the other hand, a *blue ocean*
is an uncontested market space that provides a company with room to
grow. Blue ocean strategists gaze out across the alternatives that are
available in the marketplace and create new markets of their own.

By building a fresh alternative to what was available at the time,
Southwest developed a blue ocean strategy long before the term was
coined. As Kim and Mauborgne write, "Southwest Airlines concen-
trated on driving as the alternative to flying, providing the speed of

air travel at the price of car travel and creating the blue ocean of short-haul air travel." By doing so, it developed a blue ocean from the new market it developed from the ground up:

> Southwest Airlines created a blue ocean by breaking the trade-offs customers had to make between the speed of airplanes and the economy and flexibility of car transport. To achieve this, Southwest offered high-speed transport with frequent and flexible departures at prices attractive to the mass of buyers. By eliminating and reducing certain factors of competition and raising others in the traditional airline industry, as well as by creating new factors drawn from the alternative industry of car transport, Southwest Airlines was able to offer unprecedented utility for air travelers and achieve a leap in value with a low-cost business model.[6]

They add that Southwest also "pioneered point-to-point travel between midsize cities," which changed the way the entire industry has operated since the U.S. federal government deregulated the airlines in 1978. By showing the airline industry that there is an alternative to the hub-and-spoke systems used by most of the other major airlines, Southwest opened up a new way for people to fly, as well as a new way for modern airline companies to make money. Today, passengers are no longer tied to the artificial flight patterns created by the siphoning of people into the large airlines' main hubs in cities sometimes far off a direct flight path between cities thanks to Southwest's innovative approach to air travel in the United States.

DETERMINE YOUR OWN OUTCOMES

When the coauthors of *Ordinary Greatness*, organizational development experts Pamela Bilbrey and Brian Jones, write about how people are responsible for their own outcomes, they quote best-selling author and executive consultant Jim Collins, who describes how company leaders can take ownership of their situations. In their book, Collins describes Southwest Airlines as an example of a company that has been able to succeed by taking control of its own outcomes. He points out that the airline industry has seen its share of big events and wild factors that are uncontrollable by mere managerial activities. Since 1972, Collins explains, these have included fuel shocks, spikes in federal interest rates, the deregulation of the entire industry, global armed conflicts, and the terrorist attacks of September 11, 2001.

Collins observes that "the number-one performing company of all publicly traded companies in terms of return to investors for a 30-year period from 1972 to 2002 is an airline. According to *Money* magazine's retrospective look in 2002, Southwest Airlines beat Intel, Walmart, GE—all of them!" Time and again, the leaders at Southwest have proven that their company offers a role model to companies inside and outside the airline industry.[7]

THE SOUTHWEST AIRLINES BRAND: ENERGIZED DIFFERENTIATION

In *The Brand Bubble*, marketing expert John Gerzema and branding expert Ed Lebar cite Southwest as a prime example of what they call "energized differentiation" as they describe the difference between brands that are merely strong and those that have "commanded greater usage, consideration, loyalty, and pricing power," as well as "brought greater future value through growth in operations and earnings and future stock performance." According to their studies, brands with a high level of this energized differentiation in the airline industry include Virgin Atlantic, JetBlue, and Southwest Airlines. While Virgin Atlantic was rated slightly higher than the other two airlines according to "percent of brand loyalty," Southwest surpassed both of the other airlines according to brand strength, which they call "energized differentiation and relevance."[8]

Gerzema and Lebar's data show that, despite the commoditized nature of the airline industry, "energized brands far surpass their peers." They write that "a few airlines have established relatively high levels of energy compared to their competition. These included Virgin, JetBlue, and Southwest—each in its own way highly innovative and customer focused in its business model, product and service delivery, and marketing." The authors found that all of these brands had a level of "Energized Differentiation that translated to loyalty almost twice as high as the rest of the airline category, helping them transcend the cycle of commoditization that continually plagues other airlines" such as British Airways, American Airlines, Continental Airlines, and United Airlines.[9]

When describing how companies put their "brand vision" into practice, Gerzema and Lebar explain that brands with notably strong "visions" are in the top 10 percent of all the brands they studied. They write that the visions these brands express "cut across a spectrum of benefits from making work more enjoyable for their employees to changing the world we live in."[10]

Among several companies with a notably strong vision, Southwest is cited as a prime example because "Southwest Airlines says—and means—'Employees are our first customer.'" The authors point out that one example of this is the fact that Southwest sends birthday cards to all of its employees annually. Birthday cards, celebrations, awards, recognition in employee publications, and family-like connections and support are just some of the ways that Southwest shares its strong vision with its people and keeps them motivated and engaged.

TV ADS

Both love and humor play a large role in the work of Southwest Airlines. These important ingredients in the company's success can be found throughout its culture, history, and advertising, including its television ads.

At the Smithsonian National Air and Space Museum, Herb Kelleher spoke about the company he founded and the lessons that can be learned by studying the company's work, giving a speech as part of the annual Charles A. Lindbergh Memorial Lecture series called "Kelleher: Agent of Change" on May 13, 2008. Before this speech, audience members were treated to an assortment of television advertisements from Southwest's first years of operation. In each of the ads, Kelleher jokes with the customers and puts a friendly face on the company's operations. A company jingle ends one ad, "We're Southwest Airlines, with love."[11]

While he was chairman and CEO of Southwest Airlines, Kelleher took his company and his industry to a new level of customer satisfaction when he helped to create the "ten-minute turnaround." This was promoted in a TV ad from the company's early days, in which Kelleher spoke directly to his customers and explained:

> At Southwest Airlines, we want our passengers to spend their time in the air, not on the ground. That's why we invented the ten-minute turnaround. Our planes pull into the jet-way, board passengers, and then pull out again in ten minutes or less. The way we look at it, the quicker you're in the air, the quicker you get where you're going.

The visuals of this commercial speak volumes about the message it contains. In the ad, Kelleher takes too much time talking to the camera, and the airplane begins to leave without him. Although he knocks on the airplane's door and says, "Kelleher here," the plane continues to depart. Inside the plane that has just boarded its other passengers, a flight attendant smiles and says, "You're going to love our Southwest spirit."

In another early Southwest advertisement, Kelleher appears under the banner "The Unknown Flyer," wearing a brown paper bag with two eye holes cut into it over his head (an obvious spoof of a popular comedian at the time, the Unknown Comic). "Recently, another airline suggested you might be embarrassed to fly Southwest Airlines," Kelleher says. "Well, if you're embarrassed to fly the airline with the most convenient schedules to the cities it serves, Southwest will give you

Southwest Airlines' chairman emeritus Herb Kelleher hangs on to the tail of one of Southwest's Boeing 737s featuring the company's early design for its aircraft. (Courtesy Southwest Airlines.)

this bag." He points to the bag on his head. "If you're embarrassed to fly the airline with the fewest customer complaints in the country, Southwest will give you this bag." He points to the bag again. Then he removes the bag from his head, revealing his identity, and says, "If, on the other hand, Southwest is your kind of airline, we'll still give you this bag, for all the money you'll save flying with us." As he says this, a load of dollar bills drops into the bag from above, overflowing it. The tag line reads: "Fly Southwest Airlines." The easy-to-understand humor of the advertisement, the personal approach it takes, and the willingness to face the company's detractors head-on speak volumes about the attitude of Southwest's chairman, as well as the airline's corporate philosophy.

UNIONS

The vast majority of the employees who work for Southwest Airlines—nearly 90 percent—are in a union. Embracing unions is another way that the company demonstrates its respect for its people, shows them that it cares about their welfare and well-being, and shows other companies how to work with the needs of employees who believe in collective bargaining.

Describing Southwest Airlines in their book *The New American Workplace*, James O'Toole and Edward E. Lawler III write:

> Since it was formed in the 1970s, the company has sought to avoid adversarial relations with the nine unions representing some 90 percent of its workforce. For example, when the company decided to offer employees a flexible benefits plan, it did so without forcing the unions to negotiate for it.[12]

By working with its union employees instead of incessantly fighting with them over their benefit packages, Southwest's leaders show the company's workers that they stand by the principle of always putting its internal customers—its employees—first. Working well with unions also helps the company serve as an employee-centric role model for other companies.

EMPLOYEE INVOLVEMENT

Another way Southwest Airlines shows other companies how to work with their people is by demonstrating how a company's leaders can identify problems and then form small teams of people who will help to develop solutions. O'Toole and Lawler write that, instead of controlling the company and its people with strict rules and formal hierarchical structures, Southwest Airlines "has built a consistent culture of employee involvement."[13] This employee involvement has created the breakthrough employee engagement that has become one of the most written about and copied corporate cultures in the world.

BUSINESS STRATEGY AT SOUTHWEST

In his book *The Momentum Effect*, author and business strategy expert J. C. Larreche describes Southwest Airlines as an example of a company that has mastered the concept of capitalizing on "customer lifetime value" and overcoming the "transaction myopia" that keeps companies from realizing the profit potential of long-term customers. "The key purpose of customer lifetime value." Larreche writes, "is to shift from a transaction-based mindset to a customer equity mindset, an essential element for building sustainable, profitable growth."[14]

Larreche writes that low-cost airlines have done more than just create more efficiency in their operations. They have also "exploited the transactional myopia of established airlines that traditionally gave most importance to first-class and business-class passengers because of the higher prices and margins."[15] He points out that the egalitarian nature of Southwest Airlines' operations has been a large part of the company's success:

> In the 1970s, when Southwest unveiled its low-fare strategy, the idea seemed at odds with the industry's conventional wisdom of concentrating on big tickets and long routes. Thirty years later, it is one of the world's most successful airlines. A short Southwest hop between two intrastate cities might cost about $50, a price that enables people to change their transportation habits and fly much more frequently than before. They will fly to local business meetings, to visit family, to watch a sports event, or even to commute between home and office. A commuter on such a route who flies once a week will represent an equity to SWA of about $50,000 over ten years. Suddenly the numbers begin to look pretty big despite the small value of a single transaction. This compelling equity is one of the drivers behind Southwest's momentum growth.[16]

Leaders at other airlines have much to learn from Southwest's belief in this type of compelling, long-term equity that can be gained from customers who become lifelong fans. By paying attention to lifetime customer value, Southwest has survived and thrived for nearly forty years.

Let People Act Like People

In *The Momentum Effect*, Larreche points out that many successful companies are discovering the benefits of creating company cultures that allow "employees to behave like normal human beings." He adds: "Normal human behavior happens spontaneously in companies such as Virgin, First Direct, Southwest Airlines, and Google." In other words, these companies don't over-manage their employees, since "too much management hinders the potential of the individual and confines us to expensive, growth-limiting rituals."[17] Thanks to its principles and policies that let people act like people, Southwest prospers.

Competition

Many other airline companies have tried to follow Southwest's business model but could not replicate the legendary corporate culture that helps Southwest survive and thrive. Starting in the early 1990s and continuing until recently, many of the major airlines created low-fare subsidiaries to compete directly with Southwest and other low-cost

Job Security

Consultants David Sirota, Louis A. Mischkind, and Michael Irwin Meltzer, in their book *The Enthusiastic Employee: How Companies Profit by Giving Workers What They Want*, hold up Southwest Airlines as an example of a company that has profited by using an approach that other "highly successful enterprises" have used to save money while creating enthusiastic and engaged employees: minimal layoffs.[18]

In the chapter of their book on job security, they quote Lester Thurow from MIT, who writes:

> Layoffs are painful and costly. There are numerous reasons they should be avoided if possible: Severance payments must be made. Higher training costs lie ahead. The skilled members of the team whom a firm has laid off will not be there to be rehired when times get better. Morale suffers among the remaining workers, and fewer will be willing to make personal sacrifices to help the company while it needs it most.[19]

Building morale through a sense of increased job security is just one way Southwest keeps its people happy and raises their productivity levels. A no-layoff policy also helps the company save money in the long run on recruiting, hiring, rehiring, and training.

As the coauthors of *The Enthusiastic Employee* note: "Southwest Airlines has never laid off any workers, not even after September 11, 2001. CEO James F. Parker said at the time, 'We are willing to suffer some damage, even to our stock price, to protect the jobs of our people.'"[20] Southwest has learned through decades of experience that when a company shows loyalty to its people, those people reciprocate by becoming more loyal to that company.

Sirota, Mischkind, and Meltzer point out that Southwest is unique in its field: "For example, Continental Airlines, a company very similar to Southwest in its approach to employees and in its business sector, laid off 12,000 workers in the aftermath of September 11." They explain that the real issue isn't that companies should never lay off their employees, but whether "employees see the company's decisions as balancing its immediate business interests with a consideration of how those decisions affect employees." Southwest's attitude toward its employees, they write, comes from its long-term orientation toward its people: "A significant part of its longer-term perspective is a respect for employees as assets that are not lightly disposed of."[21] Southwest's layoff policy is a highly visible way the company's leaders demonstrate their commitment to the organization's people every day.

carriers such as Frontier Airlines. For example, Delta Air Lines created a low-cost brand called Song, which operated from 2003 until 2006, and United Airlines spun off a low-cost brand called Ted, which operated from 2003 until 2009. Yet while they were able to copy the low fares, none of these airlines were able to duplicate the other elements of the Southwest model, such as its strong and vibrant corporate culture that people come from far and wide to study. None of these low-fare subsidiaries still exists today.

"You Can't Copy the People"

Southwest manager Brian Lusk says there are several things about Southwest Airlines that have made it a company from which others can learn. One of those things is the way the company treats its customers. "That's part of the Southwest culture," he says, "the way that the culture extends to our customers. You'll hear a lot of people say that anyone can copy our business model, which is flying a single type of airplane, point-to-point service with low fares. Anyone can copy that, but you can't copy the people. And I think our customers realize that."

He also points out that Southwest has been able to take the low-fare airline model, which others had tried before Southwest went into business, and improve it to make it into something new. "We're kind of like Henry Ford. He didn't invent the automobile, but he adapted the assembly line better than anyone did. We've taken the low-fare airline model and really remained true to it and adapted it better than, I think, anyone else in the country has."

Chapter Five

Satisfied Customers and Frequent Flyers

SOUTHWEST FREQUENT FLYER DR. DANIEL FINK

Daniel W. Fink, DDS, has been flying since he was a young boy. As a forty-one-year-old dentist who has pursued flying as a hobby and a passion for many years, his interest goes beyond being a Southwest frequent flyer. A few years ago, he also received his pilot's license and has been flying helicopters ever since.

When the topic of Southwest Airlines comes up, Dr. Fink lights up with enthusiasm for his favorite airline. "I have flown a decent amount over my life," he says. "My father-in-law had been using Southwest for business travel a lot, so I figured I'd try it. Everything was just so easy to deal with. The people seem like they like their jobs, and they're friendly. The whole way they do their system works for me." As a result of his positive experiences with the company, Fink says he flies on Southwest at least four or five times each year.

"Everybody's on the Same Level"

Fink says many things about the company appeal to him. "What I liked about it was the ease of use. I like the system where everybody's on the same level. If you're on the ball, you can get a good seat. If you don't really care, then you're still on the plane: It doesn't really matter. But the main thing that I liked about it was just the attitude of the employees. They just put you at ease. They're not talking down to you like you're a kid, or like you're ruining their day by just talking to them."

As a pilot himself, Fink has an insider's perspective on the ways that an airline operates. "When I'm flying Southwest, one thing I noticed was that they only fly one aircraft: the 737. They don't have to stock all of these different parts. They're really just working with one airplane, which I thought was a really cool business idea. And then I'd read that they prepurchased a bunch of fuel options for five years or so, and I thought that was a pretty good business practice, too. They did that a few years ago, and I think that's one of the things that allowed them to keep their prices low. They were able to prebuy their fuel when other people didn't. I know that other airlines were paying much more when it went up last year."

When Fink was unhappy with the other airlines that he had flown in the past, he switched to Southwest to see what the company had to offer. He says he sought out Southwest Airlines in the beginning because he was mad at one of the other airlines that had left him stranded in Florida by not letting him know that his flight back to Philadelphia had been canceled. Once he tried his first Southwest Airlines flight, he was hooked. That's when he joined Southwest's Rapid Rewards frequent flyer program. "When I started flying them, I started looking at their business practices and how they do things. I thought, this is a pretty cool company and a company I'd like to support that way. For me, from a pilot's perspective, they do some smart practices that appeal to me."

Honesty

Dr. Fink likes the honesty of a company that gives him what it says it will give him. He also enjoys the fact that he's never had to deal with the same types of problems that he had when he flew on other carriers in the past. After three years of flying on Southwest, he says he has never been delayed for the same lengths of time that he was routinely held up when he flew on Southwest's competitors. "It's unbelievable," he says. "I think the final straw was when [the other airline] canceled a flight and then I had to drive home [to Delaware] from Florida because I had to get to work the next day."

Fink also had additional problems with one of Southwest's competitors that caused him to look for an alternative carrier. He explains that this other carrier was having many difficulties: "I bought these first-class tickets, and I get there and in first class one of the seats didn't have a seatback. So, the planes were in disrepair. You could tell morale was just not good at [the other carrier]."

Fun Flights

Fink's initial flight on Southwest Airlines was a completely different story. He recalls, "My first flight, the dude giving the cabin briefing was telling jokes, and he says, 'You're supposed to wear your seatbelt the way a captain wears his thong: Tight and low across his waist,' that kind of stuff, you know, just goofy. They're fun. That makes it fun."

Passengers are put at ease when an airline's employees are demonstrably enjoying their jobs. Customers also like the benefits of using a system that helps them get what they want when they want it. Fink explains: "It's cool when you can figure out a company's system and then learn to use it, and then you get rewarded. For instance, the way they do their check-in policies, if you're on the ball and you check in right at 24 hours before the flight, you're going to get a seat in the first grouping, in the 'A' grouping, and you can get a pretty decent seat that way. Whereas, with [another carrier] I don't think I was ever sitting in the front half of the plane when I flew coach."

Southwest.com

Fink uses Southwest's Web site, www.southwest.com, to plan his travel arrangements. He says he enjoys the site's ease of use: "I use their Web site pretty much exclusively to buy my seats. I buy my seats and check in online as well." He adds that Southwest's Web site is just as easy, if not easier, to use than those of other airlines.

After three years of flying with Southwest, Fink has become a big fan of the company. "Overall, I love it. It's very convenient for me to fly from Philly to Fort Lauderdale. . . . And that would be the first airline I'd check if I were flying somewhere else."

The company's policies and people keep him coming back to Southwest: "You can tell when the captain is standing in the doorway and they're smiling and talking with the passengers. Even the gate agents are very affable and very helpful. I used to get the impression at [another carrier] like, 'How dare you talk to me. You're ruining my day. Go away, you peon!'"

Consistency

Fink appreciates the fact that Southwest flies only Boeing 737s. He says he enjoys the consistency of Southwest's service: "From one flight to another, you know what the seat layout is going to be. You pretty much know what the airplane is going to be like. You know that the likelihood of there being a parts problem is not going to be an issue because they've got a ton of parts and they're not flying different aircraft. It is also nice to see a company buying an American aircraft as opposed to a European [plane]." Although he says that he is not a protectionist consumer, the idea of a company that flies only American planes appeals to him. "It's nice. It's not a deal breaker, but it is nice."

There are many reasons Dr. Fink is such a big fan of Southwest Airlines, but one of the primary ones is that the company serves as a role model for the way a company should treat its employees. "I think that what it boils down to is the people. I've tried to incorporate that into my business, this culture of trying to be as nice as possible, like you're enjoying your job and you like being there."

FREQUENT FLYER BETH M.

Beth M., from Maryland, is also a member of Southwest Airlines' Rapid Rewards frequent flyer program. As a traveler who sometimes flies with family members who have physical disabilities, she says that she likes how these family members are treated when they are traveling on Southwest. She thinks that Southwest is "the only airline that knows how to deal with physically disabled folks." The word she uses to describe the company is "friendly." "I like how when you are stuck on the runway, someone will sing the 'Southwest' song or tell jokes. I consider them the airline with personality!" She also likes how the company deals with any problems that might occur. "They also give free drinks if your flight is delayed," she explains. "They really try to take care of you. I like them. Although flying and traveling sucks!"

LARA JEAN HAMMOND

Coffee shop owner Lara Jean Hammond, a native of Meridian, Mississippi, who runs Sage Coffee and Books there, became a fan of Southwest Airlines in the 1990s. She says it was "the most laid back and on-schedule" airline that she has ever flown. And when they did have a delay for some reason, she says, the company made up for any inconvenience with first-class treatment.

FREQUENT FLYER TERRY WEISS

Terry Weiss from suburban Philadelphia is a Southwest frequent flyer who has been a member of the airlines' Rapid Rewards program ever since Southwest Airlines started flying flights out of her local airport, Philadelphia International, seven years ago. Every year, she and her husband fly to see their son in California and her sister in Florida. "Any family function we have," she says, "I'll first go to Southwest."

Weiss explains that, before she ever stepped foot on a Southwest airplane, the company came very highly recommended: "We had heard so many [good] things about Southwest from other people who had flown them, so once they opened in Philly, we signed up for their Rapid Rewards. In general, if there's ever a flight that is available to a city [where my husband and I are traveling], we would take the Southwest flight."

Low Fares and a Unique Boarding Policy

The first thing that appealed to Weiss about Southwest's flights is that they are less expensive than those of other airlines. She also likes the fact that there are no assigned seats, which makes the turnover at the airport much faster than what she experienced when she flew with Southwest's competitors. "I like the 'first come, first served,' and they've actually modified that. It used to be A, B, and C, and then you'd still have to stand in line in your letter. But now it truly is first come, first served, and all you do is, when it's time, you just stand in line wherever your number is. So, you don't have to be there hours before or stand in line for a long time. It usually works out that the first 60 [passengers] are A, and it goes 1 to 60; and it's B, 61 to 120, so you know where you're going to be. You just walk on the plane and you take whatever seat you want."

Weiss prefers Southwest's new boarding protocol as "a refinement of the original Southwest seating" because it means that she no longer has to stand in line before flights for as long as she did previously. "If I know I'm A-30, when it's time for the A's, I just get up and find my place."

She finds the company's boarding policy "very logical." "If you don't have assigned seating, things get done faster. And I can understand, by not having that, that's a computer system that you don't have to pay for. It's cutting costs, but not in a bad way."

On November 8, 2007, Southwest Airlines streamlined its boarding process, eliminating "cattle calls" and the need to "camp out" when waiting in line to board its flights, by introducing boarding groups (A, B, and C) and boarding numbers (in groups of five). (Courtesy Southwest Airlines.)

An Outstanding Safety Record and Fewer Fees

Along with the company's low fares and its egalitarian boarding policy, another thing about Southwest that appeals to Weiss is the company's outstanding safety record. "Normally you don't hear about them in crashes," she says.

She also likes that Southwest Airlines is one of the few airlines that does not charge its customers for their first two checked bags. She says that the lower fees speak volumes about how the company treats its customers: "I think that shows you what they're like. There's no fee if you change your flight. A lot of airlines charge you, which now might be up as high as $150, if something comes up and you have to change your flight. Southwest does not charge you."

"A Little Kooky"

Weiss's experiences while aboard Southwest's aircraft have been more pleasant than her flights on other airlines. She has found that Southwest's flight attendants interact with customers in a very different way than those of other airlines with which she's flown and feels that's a good thing. She says that sometimes they are "a little kooky, which is fine. These people, they will make jokes."

As a regular traveler, Weiss says she really doesn't mind if there is an occasional problem, but she just likes to know that the airline is aware of the problem and doing everything it can to fix it. "Sometimes if there is a problem leaving or coming in, I find that they usually are pretty good about letting you know." This is why she likes Southwest: The company keeps passengers aware of what's happening behind the scenes.

She adds that she believes that Southwest Airlines is better at following its schedule than most other airlines on which she has flown in the past. "I've also felt that they were more on time," Weiss says.

Patience

Another aspect of her experience with Southwest Airlines that Terry Weiss says she enjoys is the level of patience that the company's employees show to her as a passenger. She says there is also something "calming" about how the pilots at Southwest make humorous comments over the aircraft's intercom about the city where they are landing, the weather, and even the air traffic controllers.

Weiss knows from experience that Southwest is different from its competitors. Before Southwest Airlines flew out of Philadelphia International Airport, she flew other airlines, on which she had several problems. Now, if she has a choice between a one-stop flight to California from Philadelphia on Southwest or a nonstop flight on another airline, she and her husband will choose Southwest, even though it is somewhat longer, because she knows she will have a better experience. When she recently took this option, she said it was well worth it, even though she had to stay on the airplane while some passengers got off and others got on when the plane stopped at its first destination. She said the time of her wait was very reasonable. "It was maybe twenty or twenty-five minutes, if that much, between people getting off and people getting on. It was a very short amount of time." To pass the time, she and several of the other passengers who were waiting simply walked up and down the aisles of the airplane to stretch their legs.

Lower Costs Overall

To deal with the fact that Southwest does not serve meals on its flights, Weiss says she and her husband simply bring their own food and enjoy the free drinks that are served on the plane. "That's another thing," she adds, "if you don't have it, you don't have the expense."

Weiss says that she simply thinks of these differences about Southwest as part of the savings that the company passes along to its customers, which help to keep its fares so low. Weiss estimates that she usually saves about 30 percent on her flights compared to other airlines when she buys her tickets with Southwest online at www.southwest.com.

Those low fares are the key to Weiss's commitment to Southwest Airlines as her airline of choice. When she recommends the airline to her friends or family members, she says she also boasts about the company's ability to keep its flights punctual. "Most of the time," she says, "they are on time, if not earlier." Her one complaint about Southwest is that the airline does not fly to as many cities as other airlines, but she says she has noticed that more cities are being added to its schedule every year.

Chapter Six

Love, Freedom, and Southwest's Corporate Practices

SPREADING LOVE

In 1971, the first year of operations for Southwest Airlines (represented by the letters LUV on the New York Stock Exchange), the company started its first advertising campaign, with love as a central theme.

An advertisement in the first issue of *Southwest Airlines* magazine in 1971 featured the headline "How Do We Love You? Let Us Count the Ways." The ad simply posted the entire flight schedule for Southwest's flights between Dallas, San Antonio, and Houston, along with graphics of a heart and a Boeing 737. Under the name of the company, a tiny tag line read, "The Somebody Else Up There Who Loves You."

By 1977, Southwest was beginning to fly to more cities throughout Texas. An advertisement that year from the company stated, "We're Spreading Love All over Texas." It went on to describe how the company was spreading its service all around the state, including Dallas, Houston, San Antonio, the Rio Grande Valley, Corpus Christi, Lubbock, El Paso, Midland/Odessa, and Austin. The simple ad once again showed a graphic depiction of an airplane flying, but this time it cast its shadow across most of the state. Nine hearts rest on the shape of Texas, representing the new cities where the airline would be flying. The copy explains, "Bringing low fares, good times, free drinks and beautiful service to the most convenient airports in Texas! That's love on Southwest Airlines and we're spreading it around."[1]

Spreading love was an unusual selling point for an airline at the time, but it worked. People fell in love with the company that wasn't afraid to give that love right back to them in its messages and its "fun-LUVing" attitude.

More Love

As a demonstration of its commitment to the theme of love in its branding, Southwest Airlines unveiled a new corporate logo in 2002.

The company replaced the orange, red, and gold stripes that appeared under "Southwest" with a new and more loving image.

Today, the airline's logo is made up of a gold circle in which its name, "Southwest Airlines," appears in the same sky blue as the background color. On top of this circle are two gold wings. In the center of it all is the outline of a prominent red heart. With this change, the airline that started at Love Field with the LUV stock ticker code placed its love for its employees and its customers front and center in its new logo and corporate message. Cynthia Hill, Southwest's director of advertising, explains, "Southwest Airlines has a distinct personality, humor and a big heart. We see ourselves as a caring, loving company—a company of people, not planes."[2]

As Southwest founder Herb Kelleher has said in the past, planes are tangible, but a people-centric spirit is a vital intangible. By putting its people and the emotions that connect them before all else—in its logo and in its corporate policies—Southwest has become a company that is much more than the sum of its physical property and products.

Love at LUV

While every employee at Southwest has his or her reason for coming into work every day, one thing that comes up again and again when talking to them is their mutual love of their company.

As an employee who worked at another airline before coming to Southwest, Manager of Online Relationships and Special Projects Brian Lusk says that he has very strong emotions toward the company where he now works: "I love working here. I've worked here fourteen years and I worked at Delta eighteen and a half. Towards the end of my time at Delta, it was just a drudgery to come to work. I absolutely hated it.

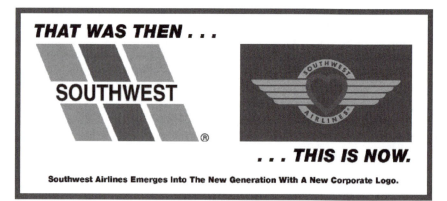

In 2002, Southwest Airlines adopted a new company logo. (Courtesy Southwest Airlines.)

When I came to work at Southwest, I started at our Reservations Center. It was actually fun. It was fun being around people. It was great to work at a place where your efforts are appreciated, or you're considered an individual, and the individual matters. And, as I've gone through into different positions, I've also been lucky enough to find the kind of work that I really enjoy."

Lusk has a degree in fine arts and was a journalism major. After graduation, he found that he had drifted away from those early passions into another area in which he was also really interested: the airline industry. After many years of working for Delta Air Lines and then coming over to Southwest, Lusk says that he feels that his new company allows him to combine his talent for writing with his experience with working in the airline industry. "Now I'm kind of in the area where I can combine both of those, so I enjoy the actual work that I do, too."

IDEA CITY

Roy Spence is the CEO and cofounder of the advertising agency GSD&M, which changed its name to GSD&M Idea City in 2007. One of GSD&M Idea City's top clients is Southwest Airlines, and the work it has done for the carrier has helped to create its unique image in the world.

In his blog, Bill Taylor, the author of *Mavericks at Work*, writing about the creativity of Spence, declared that the ad agency's founder had produced some of the most memorable ads in history, including those for its "signature client" Southwest Airlines. Taylor credits this to his ability to see beyond the company's slogans and into the ideas the company represents. Taylor says that Spence tries to express a company's purpose with the advertisements he creates. Taylor quotes Spence: "Anybody who's running a business has to seek out the higher calling of that business, its purpose. Purpose is about the difference you're trying to make—in the marketplace, in the world." Spence adds, "If everybody is selling the same thing, what's the tie-breaker? It's purpose."[3]

Taylor continues:

Southwest is not in the low-fare airline business, Roy Spence insists. It is in the freedom business. Its purpose is to democratize the skies—to make air travel as accessible for average Americans as for the well-to-do. "Would you rather be in the airline business or the freedom business?"[4]

Spence calls everyone who works for Southwest a "freedom fighter," Taylor explains, because they work together to provide the American

Freedom

Southwest Airlines' belief in the power of freedom plays a role in the company's advertising, its employee policies, and its recruiting practices when seeking new people. In 2000, when it was looking for new recruits to join its expanding ranks, Southwest ran an ad that featured a prominent smiley face made out of peanuts above a tag line that said, "The Freedom to be yourself is the freedom to be your best. Log on for great career opportunities at southwest.com." The advertisement went on to say that the people of Southwest "believe people do their best work when they have the freedom to be who they are."

public with the freedom to fly for lower fares. This type of story captures hearts and sells tickets.

NO LAYOFFS AFTER A BIG LOSS

While the theme of freedom can be used during boom times to help a company grow, it can also be used during tough economic times to help a company shrink its workforce. Many airlines shrink their employee levels by issuing mandatory furloughs; in other words, they lay off numerous workers in one fell swoop. But Southwest takes a different route: Instead of issuing mandatory furloughs, the company gives its people the freedom to choose whether or not they leave the company when times are tight.

For example, on April 17, 2009, Southwest faced bad news. The recession that had started at the end of 2008 continued to ground more and more businesspeople and leisure travelers. Feeling the effects of declining fuel prices on its fuel-hedging program as well as the declining number of people who were flying to their destinations, Southwest reported a "surprisingly large quarterly loss," which Southwest CEO Gary C. Kelly said was due to "the toughest revenue environment in our history."[5] Although the company had posted steady profits for more than seventeen years in a row, the loss was the third quarterly drop in net profit for the company. According to Reuters, the company lost $91 million during the first quarter of 2009. A year earlier, the company had posted a profit of $34 million.

Southwest was not the only company to suffer during the same quarter. Virtually all airlines were hit hard by the recession. For example, AMR Corp., the parent company of American Airlines, posted a quarterly loss of $375 million the day before Southwest announced its own bad news.

What makes Southwest different from other companies is that, given this tough revenue environment, instead of choosing to lay off its workforce, the company instead decided to offer its 35,500 employees buyouts for the third time since 2004. Rather than forcing people to leave the company, Southwest's leaders gave each employee the freedom to decide whether he or she wanted to stay or take the company's voluntary buyout offer, which included a cash payout, health care coverage, and some flight benefits based on the length of time the employee had been with the company.

Years earlier, when the company closed a couple of its reservations centers, instead of issuing mandatory furloughs, Southwest offered its employees either a buyout package or relocation to another reservation center. At that time, 1,500 employees accepted the buyouts.

In April 2009, the company also said it planned to cut capital spending over the next few years to cope with the loss. Another way the company dealt with the bad news was instilling a hiring freeze across the company and freezing the pay for top executives and senior managers.

BILL OWEN

Today, when Southwest schedules its flights across its sixty-eight cities in thirty-five states, the company works hard to offer its customers the maximum number of choices of times and destinations while balancing these with the limitations and restrictions of the company's employees and resources. Giving Southwest's passengers the most freedom to fly when and where they want to, while keeping the airline productive and profitable is a challenge that Bill Owen faces every day.

Owen is the lead planner in Southwest's Schedule Planning Department, which operates the company's point-to-point schedule, which is very different from the hub-and-spoke systems used by most other airlines. Within Southwest's unique system, Owen's department is responsible for writing the schedules for more than 3,300 flights every single day.

"It truly is a mind-boggling task to juggle aircraft and market demand," explains Brian Lusk, "and Bill is an expert on this."

Owen has worked for the company for more than nineteen years and has served for years on Southwest's Corporate Culture Committee. He is also one of Southwest's most prolific bloggers on *Nuts About Southwest* (www.blogsouthwest.com), the company's corporate Web log. Not only does he write about the work he does within the company, but he has also created a dedicated following for his posts by writing about nearly every other aspect of his personal and professional life.

When asked about his years with Southwest Airlines, Owen exclaims, "It's a great company!"

Owen started his work in the airline industry many years before he was hired by Southwest Airlines. He worked for American Airlines for ten years, where he started in the Reservations Department and moved into schedule planning after he received a marketing degree and the company moved its headquarters to Fort Worth, Texas, from New York.

He resigned from his position at American when he went into the trucking business with his father. After managing that company for three years, he was ready for a change. That's when he sought a job with Southwest Airlines. "Trust me," he laughs, "don't ever go to work for your parents. It just does not work!"

Owen says he missed working in the airline industry, but he wanted to work for a company other than American: "I had been there, done that, had the T-shirt."

Revenue Management

When he saw a job opening at Southwest, Owen applied for the job. After a series of interviews, he was hired in the Revenue Management Department in 1990. He describes it as a "department that most consumers love to hate. It's their job to make sure they extract as much revenue out of every flight as they can, and they do that by monitoring incoming bookings and traffic levels and then adjusting discounts, seat inventory, and fare prices accordingly."

Scheduling Thousands of Flights Each Day

Owen says that it was always his goal to get into Southwest's Schedule Planning Department once he joined Southwest, but since the company rarely hires people from outside the company for that department, he bided his time in revenue management until an opening presented itself. He explains that schedule planning "is a very interesting department at any airline because you know all the state secrets. You know everything that's being looked at and you can see exactly what's happening and what's being thought of for the future, good and bad." With his experience from another airline, he was anxious to get back to the work he had enjoyed in the past.

Today, as lead planner in Southwest's Schedule Planning Department, Owen's work group is responsible for writing and publishing the airline's schedule. This includes what every airplane does every single day, the number of flights that fly in and out of each market, and the departure times for all of them. His job is to optimize capacity, traffic, and revenue generation for all of the company's flights throughout the country.

"Various groups within the department are responsible for looking at new cities and doing analyses and proposals to expand Southwest's brand to new destinations," Owen explains. These expansions include those to LaGuardia, which took place on June 28, 2009. Other new Southwest terminal openings that took place in 2009 include Minneapolis; Boston's Logan Airport; and Milwaukee, Wisconsin.

Capacity Planning

Owen explains that schedule planning for Southwest is very different than it is for other types of airlines: "There are similarities and differences. If the question is about capacity planning, it's the same question here as it is at Continental, as it is at American: Do we need to add service in this market or do we need to take it away, and if so, about what time do we want the new service to go? Or, if we're going to cut, which flight do we want to cut? If you get at that high level of the process, the function is the same, pretty much, at any airline."

There are two things that make Southwest Airlines' operation unique. The first is Southwest's network structure, which is quite different from the hub-and-spoke systems that other airlines use to run their operations. The second thing that makes the company different, Owen says, "is the fact that everything is not reduced to a dollar sign. Although dollar signs and forecasting calculations do play a big part in it, at Southwest we're all about our brand and maximizing the effectiveness of the brand. In order to do that, you've got to acquiesce. Not every single flight in every market is going to wind up being profitable for you."

An Equitable Tradeoff

Owen says that Southwest is willing and able to forgo making a profit on a few of its flights in order to satisfy those customers who keep the business profitable with their other ticket purchases. For example, there is a dedicated group of around thirty to forty passengers who regularly fly between Las Vegas and Reno at 6 A.M. Owen says the company often does not turn a profit on that flight, "but because we know our customer base, because they've told us that they want that flight—'Don't get rid of that flight'—we leave it in. Other carriers don't have the luxury of doing that."

He continues: "We firmly believe that we wind up getting back from that in terms of brand loyalty and the fact that they're going to fly us on something else. I mean, we're not the only ones out there that they can choose. If they're going to choose us to fly from Las Vegas to Chicago because they commute with us every day from Vegas to Reno, then in our book, that's an equitable tradeoff."

NETWORK STRUCTURE

One thing that makes Southwest Airlines so unique is its linear network structure, as opposed to the hub-and-spoke systems used by most other large airlines. Southwest Airlines' system is also different from the point-to-point systems at other low-fare carriers such as Ryanair, which flies throughout Europe, and Allegiant Air, which flies to around sixty North American cities. Owen explains: "Even though you could, in theory, connect on them and go from, let's say Allentown, Pennsylvania, to Las Vegas, change planes, and then fly from Las Vegas to Fresno, California, they don't even sell that." He says that many of these carriers actually discourage connections to other flights by requiring passengers to buy a separate ticket for each leg of the flight and by not transferring bags between flights for customers. "You're responsible for getting yourself there. And if they're delayed, too bad for you. That's the definition of a true 'point-to-point' network," says Owen.

Southwest's Flight Network

At most airlines, a hub-and-spoke network involves a spider web design that connects all of the carrier's flights to a single hub at the center, through which most of that airline's flights pass. Some carriers might have two or three hubs, but the idea is the same.

Southwest's network is different. Bill Owen describes the company's flight network as "linear." He says you should think of a grid that is "maybe ten by ten—ten rows down, ten rows across." Imagine a dot at the intersection of each of those lines on the grid. A hub-and-spoke carrier would connect all of those dots only to their single hub. "Our goal," Owen says, "is to connect every single one of those dots to every single other dot, either with a single line, denoting a nonstop flight, or at least two of them together, so that you could go from A to B to C but stay on the same airplane."

Owen continues: "While we do publish connections, we don't actively schedule to them. Connections tend to happen at Southwest just because of the density of our market." This "density" is a point of differentiation that makes Southwest unique from all other airlines. Each day, Southwest Airlines flies more flights, on average, in and out of its terminals than any other airline. "For example," says Owen, "we've got twenty-seven flights a day between Dallas and Houston. That's more nonstops in that single market than any airline in the world has. And we've got a huge number of flights within the state of California. Markets like LAX [Los Angeles] to San Francisco, Burbank to Oakland, San Diego to Sacramento, core business markets of which we'll have upwards of ten, twelve, fifteen flights a day. Because we have markets with that kind of frequency, that kind of depth, you don't have to really schedule two connections. They just happen."

Southwest has a flight leaving just about every hour in its busy markets. This means the chances are good that whenever a passenger is flying from St. Louis to Dallas, for example, Southwest is going to have a flight available within an hour that is connecting to San Antonio or Austin or Houston. This kind of frequency of flights per market gives customers more freedom to fly where they want to go. It also helps to differentiate Southwest Airlines from its field of competitors.

Capabilities

As lead planner, Owen keeps close track of how many airplanes Southwest is flying when he is developing Southwest's flight schedule: "We have three different variants of 737s, and each one of them has different capabilities. You've got to know how many of each you have, and you've got to know what they can do. But, by and large, the fact that we only have one kind of airplane makes my job much, much easier. Which is good, because the fact that we are linear and not hub-and-spoke makes my job much, much, much more difficult."

Owen explains that planners at hub-and-spoke carriers only need to figure out the farthest point from the airline's main airport—its hub—and the earliest departure time that they want to allow. With this knowledge, they can figure out what time they want their airplanes to arrive at the hub. Once they have figured out the frequencies of their flights, writing the schedule for these types of airlines is easier than at Southwest, which has no hubs. "What's difficult for those guys is the fleet assignment, because you're having to deal with airplanes that range in size from anywhere from thirty seats to four hundred."

Although planners at Southwest don't have to worry about the complexity of such drastic extremes of fleet variability, they do have many other types of variables with which to contend. "We're not just flying from a whole bunch of places to a very few hub points. We're serving twenty-five, thirty, forty destinations from some of our bigger stations. But even from some littler stations, like Austin or San Antonio or Oklahoma City, we're flying to six or seven different places." Owen notes that his job includes getting the departure times optimal for the demand at each one of those markets. "Then you've got to string everything together so that you have a cohesive, operable network that doesn't exceed the number of airplanes that you've got to work with." This can make his job very difficult.

Optimization

When Owen started working in the Schedule Planning Department at Southwest, all of the calculations for creating optimal departure times to meet market demands were done manually, without the help of the optimization computer software that most airlines use today. The complexity of Southwest's network was beyond the capability of the most advanced optimization software available at the time. "It's only been in the past five years that we've been able to bring optimization to the Schedule Planning Department," says Owen.

While searching for an airline schedule optimizer, planners at Southwest found that there was no outside vendor with the capabilities they needed to help them with their flight schedule. "We actually went to one think tank that was looking at this, and we had given the guy all the prep work and he had studied our schedule and he goes, 'Well, I've got good news and bad news. The good news is that I know how big your problem is. The number of possible variations that would be in a valid Southwest schedule, given the constraints that you just identified to me, is a number that would be ten to the twenty-third power.' My boss at the time said, 'What's the bad news?' And he goes, 'We can't solve it for you.' "

To find a solution to their problem, Southwest's schedule planners considered hiring more people with the mathematical background necessary to work with such large numbers of variables. It was about this time, in January 2001, that one of Southwest's employees from its technology group showed the planners a program that could output a schedule that seemed like it might work. Owen recalls, "We're like, 'This is great! Which vendor did this?' and he said, 'I did it.' " This Southwest employee had bought an optimization license and the optimization engine called CPLEX on his own credit card and installed it on his home computer. At night after work, on weekends, and across holiday periods, that employee figured out how to create the calculations that worked.

Since then, Southwest's people have created a newer and more efficient optimization engine, which helps Southwest's planners schedule the company's flights across its system. In other words, Southwest has solved its unique problems by enlisting its unique people to use their unique talents to come up with a unique, proprietary solution.

"Our network is so different," Owen says. "Everything about Southwest is different. The way we do business is different. Our fare philosophy is different. We're not like the other guys who charge what the market can bear. We charge what we think is fair. That's why we've gone in and lowered fares. We pull people off the freeways. We pull people in from other airports. We grow markets that we go into, just exponentially. But yet another way in which we're different is self-reliance in the way that we schedule. We took a very difficult network to schedule, and by employing people that got to know the network and its nuances, they were able to do what all the eggheads at IBM's Watson Labs up in Auerbach, New York, couldn't do. But our own people could."

Southwest not only benefits financially from its policy of putting its employee first, it also benefits from the innovations and technologies its highly motivated employees develop thanks to the support they receive from their leaders and peers.

Advantages

There are a number of advantages for Southwest in scheduling its flights the way that it does. The first is maximizing productivity of every asset, from planes to personnel to location. For example, a hub-and-spoke airline will have a massive airport complex with sixty gates at which sixty airplanes will arrive at about the same time. These airplanes will often sit at the terminal for an hour or more, and then they will all leave around the same time. This means that these airlines cannot use their gates as frequently as Southwest does. "We use our gates upwards of fifteen times per day, on average," Owen notes with pride. "I don't think there's another airline in the country that can say that."

This increased frequency of flights gives Southwest the freedom to use its employees more efficiently. "You can handle the same number of flights with fewer people because, instead of having these enormous work peaks and then having absolutely nothing going on during the interim, you've got flights coming and going at a rapid clip so that your people are working a flight, and they're running over, and ten minutes later they're working another flight, and after that one push, you've got another flight coming in. You keep your people much, much busier."

While Southwest keeps its employee's busier than those who work for most of its competitors, it also rewards them with higher wages than almost any other airline. Employees also receive some of the best health coverage in the industry as well. In addition, they get free standby flights for themselves, their children, their parents, and their spouses. And, as mentioned before, job security is another part of being a Southwest employee. While other airlines have had to lay off workers to stay profitable in a rapidly shifting economy, Southwest has never had layoffs throughout its nearly forty years in operation.

Owen explains that keeping its employees productive through efficient scheduling practices helps Southwest stay profitable. "Even though we're paying them, by far, the highest wages in the industry, it averages out to where you are so much more productive that you're keeping your costs low."

Minimal Turn Times

"Turn time" is the amount of time an airplane is scheduled to be on the ground from when it lands to when it takes off again. Southwest

Airlines keeps its gates fully used by minimizing the number of gates it operates at any one time and by working hard to minimize the time between one departing flight and the next flight's arrival at the same gate. The airline also keeps its turn times very low.

As Bill Owen notes, this saves money. "If you're coming into [Dallas-Fort Worth Airport] on American, let's say, your airplane might sit on the ground for forty-five minutes. It might sit on the ground for an hour. It might sit on the ground for two hours before it loads up and goes again. An airplane that's on the ground is just inherently not making money for you. It's not generating any revenue. So, what we've discovered is that if you keep your turn times minimal, then you can have the airplane be more productive."

Eliminate "Red-Eyes"

Another important distinction between Southwest Airlines and most of its competitors is that it has eliminated from its schedule the traditional "red-eye" flights that travel through the latest hours of the night. Planning flights at times when people want to travel makes its people, planes, and gates more productive. This is part of the "less is more" philosophy that keeps prices at Southwest so low.

While other airlines schedule overnight, red-eye flights from coast to coast, Southwest doesn't believe in scheduling flights at times when very few passengers will be flying, for two reasons:

1. *Employees.* Southwest doesn't want to subject its crews to such grueling work conditions. This is a quality-of-life issue.
2. *Customers.* Leaders at Southwest Airlines understand that customers do not want to fly at those times. "If they can get an absolute rock-bottom deal, they'll take it, but they're going to complain and grumble," Owen believes. He points out that they don't call these flights red-eyes for nothing. "You get there and your eyes are all red and you're cranky and tired. We don't do that."

As a result, the average operating day—from the time when an airplane has its first departure of the day to the time it terminates its operations at night—is shorter at Southwest than at other airlines that fly around the clock with flights on the margins of the day that many customers do not enjoy. "We're compressing our operating day to stay in that sweet spot," says Owen.

That "sweet spot" is where Southwest's planners know there is demand for the company's services and where they know they can schedule people to keep its airplanes moving and its people productive. Owen adds, "We're also maximizing our market penetration."

New Loading Procedures

Southwest has made a name for itself in the airline business by creating a new way to load its planes with passengers. By allowing passengers to pick their own seats, Southwest created an egalitarian system in which there are no "first-class" and "coach" distinctions between customers.

Some critics of Southwest's boarding procedures have called this type of loading system a "cattle-call boarding system." So to respond to a shifting marketplace and changing customer demands, CEO Gary Kelly introduced a new system for passenger boarding in late 2007. The new boarding process continued to allow passengers to pick their seats, but instead of all passengers simply getting in line for a first-come, first-seated process, the modified system opens up an online check-in process twenty-four hours before each flight's departure time. Passengers are assigned to one of three groups, according to the order they check in online. The first passengers to check in are assigned to group A, the next group is designated as group B, and the last group of passengers to check in is assigned to group C. (Passengers with children four years old or younger are assigned to groups A and B.) When these passengers arrive at the airport, video monitors announce when it is time for each group to board the airplane.

Every passenger is also given a boarding number that tells him or her which "column" he or she is in. A column is a group of five passengers that stands near the gate by a physical column labeled with those boarding numbers. When the gate agent announces the group that is to board, those five people are allowed to move through the jet bridge together.

These changes in passenger-loading procedures are the first of their kind for any airline. Although sometimes confusing for first-time users, the new procedures have also proven to be very successful. To help passengers figure out Southwest's unique system, the company's Web site, www.southwest.com, offers a simple online "Boarding School 101" notebook and cheat sheet.

Less Is More

"We need some ways to consistently replace value-destroying complexity with value-creating simplicity," writes Matthew May in his recent book *In Pursuit of Elegance*.[6] At Southwest, this principle seems to be at work every day. By offering low-cost, no-frills flights on which complex problems such as in-flight meals, onboard movies, and class sections in seating are eliminated in favor of simpler solutions such as prepackaged snacks, plastic boarding cards, and no reserved seating, Southwest has embraced the idea that less is sometimes more.

Although it was founded on the less-is-more philosophy, the company is still willing to make changes that add a little complexity to its system to keep up with changes in the marketplace. This is why CEO Gary Kelly was able to reconsider the simplistic first-come, first-served, no-reserved-seating policy and replace it with a system in which passengers can go online twenty-four hours before their flights to receive a boarding group in which they will board the plane with several other passengers.

While some longtime customers might see this as an inconvenient addition of complexity in the system, many others have embraced the new system and enjoy the fact that they no longer have to wait in long lines. Where they once had to leave their bags unattended as placeholders in line if they needed to use a restroom, they no longer have to worry about losing their spot if they leave the line for whatever reason. Although the change involved a few additional procedures, the end result is a simple solution to a variety of different problems.

AN EFFICIENT OPERATION

Everything Southwest does, including the new boarding arrangement, is designed to facilitate fast passenger turnarounds and a very efficient operation. As scheduler Bill Owen explains, "That's everything from the way that we board to the way we load the airplane to the fact that we only fly one equipment type so that everybody that works here that's going to be touching that airplane knows exactly what they're doing. There is no ambiguity."

Another way that Southwest has streamlined its approach to air travel is by eliminating any type of elaborate onboard food service. Instead, the company simply offers its passengers a variety of prepackaged snacks, including its world-famous peanuts. Today, more and more of their competitors have done away with the meals that once were standard on all major airlines. Southwest's efficiency is catching on and continues to set trends among competitors around the globe.

Peanuts

The company prides itself on the millions of peanuts it gives to its customers. In 2006, according to *Bloomberg News*, Southwest distributed 94 million packets of peanuts to its passengers. Southwest offers peanuts on all of its flights, unless somebody on board has a severe peanut allergy.

Working with the peanut theme has become a science at Southwest Airlines, which includes peanuts—as well as its efforts to keep costs down—in its advertising, describing ticket prices as "peanuts." According to the *Dallas Morning News*, "In 2000, the airline had its vendor remove three nuts from each bag to save $300,000 a year."[7]

While Southwest might take pride in selling tickets for "peanuts," Owen says that Southwest does not cut back on the essentials. While the company has an extremely efficient operation, he explains, "We have a very nice selection of beverages available onboard. The only thing you have to pay for is alcoholic beverages. We do have a large snack selection. They're free."

No Baggage Fees

In the marketing magazine *Advertising Age*, Mya Frazier published a piece on November 18, 2008, she called "Southwest Airlines: A Marketing 50 Case Study." While discussing the large fees that more and more airlines are charging for extras that were once free, such as checked baggage, she comments on the fact that Southwest is not charging for a first or second bag: "The nickel-and-dime pricing that runs rampant in the cash-strapped airline industry is the bane of frugal travelers and a boon for Southwest Airlines."[8]

She explains that Southwest is capitalizing on its effort to keep costs low for consumers with an advertising campaign called "Freedom from Fees" that is being run from the advertising firm GSD&M Idea City, in Austin, Texas. In her article, Frazier quotes Kevin Krone, vice president of marketing, sales, and distribution at Southwest, who says, "It became very personal for people when it started getting into luggage. It was instantly a way to differentiate us from the rest of the industry."

Frazier writes that, at the end of 2008, "Southwest's commitment to economical flying continues to keep the carrier cruising above much of the turbulence. The airline's revenue rose 8.5 percent last year to $9.9 billion; for the first three quarters of 2008, revenue tracked upward 12.5 percent." Although Southwest's fortunes dipped after this period as a result of the economic recession, the airline's no-fee baggage policy may have been resonating with travelers when other airlines were beginning to charge fees for previously free services.

"All of It Works Together"

There is no elaborate in-flight entertainment on a Southwest flight. While there are no movies or video screens onboard, all of Southwest's airplanes will offer inexpensive wi-fi service to customers in the near future. Another aspect of the Southwest experience that sets it apart from its competitors is the fact that its 737s are equipped with spacious leather seats.

Low-fare does not mean low quality at Southwest. "It's not a bare-bones operation," declares Owen. "It's very comfortable. The amount of space that our seats have between them, the legroom, is above industry standards. It's a very comfortable operation. But then what really makes a difference is the people. By and large, when you check in at a Southwest gate, or you get on a Southwest airplane, chances are, you're going to be dealing with people that are happy, that are glad they have jobs in this company, and that are not afraid to smile and say, 'How are you? Thanks for flying us! What can I do for you?' You might even get a couple of jokes cracked or have a rap song sung to you or something done to you. It's that kind of a quirky place."

Success is something that happens at Southwest because of the precise combination of many factors that combine to form a unique and profitable business model. In Owen's opinion, "All of it works together. That's why everybody is so worried about changing the business model to any major degree because this all works. It all kind of hangs together. If you start wholesale monkeying with it, it's the whole unraveling-the-sweater thing. You might start with a thread on the bottom of it, and pretty soon your left arm falls off."

Be Yourself

Owen says that he believes the fact that Southwest puts its employees first is the key to its success. He likes the fact that people are not forced into molds as Southwest. "We're not forced to be clones. People are not only *allowed*, they're *encouraged* to be themselves."

By allowing people to be themselves, Southwest helps its employees to get to know each other better than they would if they worked somewhere else that might stifle their individuality. "You get to know the people that you're actually working with as people," says Owen, "not just as somebody that's working a four-day trip with you, or some guy that's sitting in a cube across the thing. You get to know the people."

Getting to know your coworkers on a professional level is one thing, but Southwest takes its employee culture to the next step. "Once you've crossed that hurdle, then you start caring about them as people. To encourage that, the company has all these avenues and venues that allow you to get involved," Owen explains.

One of the ways that people learn to connect with their coworkers at Southwest is the company's famous Culture Committee. The people who make up the Culture Committee have been picked from the employees who have been active in their local workplaces. These are the people who connect with their fellow employees by throwing barbeques, celebrating birthdays, and engendering the family spirit in a multitude of ways, both subtly and overtly.

Perpetuating the Culture

Southwest doesn't take this family spirit for granted. Owen explains, "The company actually invested a significant amount of money to foster that by teaching people how important it is." Part of that investment is bringing the Culture Committee together four times each year in Dallas to discuss what has been working to make Southwest's company culture stronger and what has not been working. After attending each meeting, the Culture Committee members go back into the field and put what they have learned into action.

Owen admits that he didn't get it at first. When he first started at Southwest, he thought all of his coworkers' talk about corporate culture was "really kind of weird." After working for another airline company where different divisions within the company were often at odds with one another and there was much animosity between certain departments, the family spirit of Southwest's corporate culture took him by surprise. But then he met a coworker who told him to get involved. "He said, 'If you get involved and understand what this is all about,' he goes, 'you'll never want to stop.' And that's exactly what I did," Owen recalls.

The Giving Spirit

Soon Owen was volunteering to help decorate the hangar with decorations for the company's Christmas party. Then he was volunteering to cook dinner at the Ronald McDonald House in Dallas, which is one of Southwest's many corporate charities. Then he was serving hamburgers to employees working the luggage ramp in Albuquerque, New Mexico, when temperatures were reaching 110 degrees. "By doing, you learn," Owen says, "and you learn what the giving spirit is all about. But then you also meet all these other people who are kind of in it for the same thing."

The connections made between coworkers during corporate charity dinners and other types of events for which employees can volunteer go deeper than the simple professional interactions that take place during formal business hours. Stronger and longer-lasting relationships are built between people when they work shoulder to shoulder while helping others who need help, whether they are sick children or coworkers who have to work on a busy holiday.

"Internalize It"

Owen discovered the power of Southwest's corporate culture by engulfing himself in it and making it part of his life, both while he is working and during his time off. "It's really a message of, if you don't make the effort to internalize it, it's going to stay superficial. That's the goal from the day you're hired, is to get you to internalize it." He adds, "Southwest Airlines is not for everybody. We have a lot of people that get here and they either don't make it off probation or they decide this is not for them, and they leave. And that's OK. But if you get here and you do internalize it, and you do embrace the culture, then it gives you so much."

For example, when Owen's mother died, nearly a quarter of the people who attended her funeral were people who had never met her. They were Southwest employees from throughout the company who worked with her son. "They were there to support me," Owen says, "and to celebrate, basically, all the beefy stories that I had told them about my mom over the years. It's that kind of place."

FAMILY

As a result of Southwest's corporate culture and many, many personal and professional interactions in and out of the workplace, Bill Owen says he has gained more than friends at Southwest: These people are family. "Friends are wonderful, but family will always be there. Even if they're mad at you, they'll always be there for you. That's what this is like."

As a member of a very large extended biological family that has a family reunion every year with more than two hundred people in attendance, Owen understands what family is all about. He says that he figured out "that whole family thing" almost immediately after he started to work at Southwest because he'd been exposed to it his entire life.

While most of Southwest's employees have created outstanding careers for themselves by working within Southwest's unique, family-like corporate culture, there are always a few people who don't get it. "There are people that come here and think, 'Oh yeah, this culture thing is just all one big party. Let's get together on Friday and have a beer or two.' Well, that's not it at all. That's only a tiny piece of it. That's getting together and sharing and talking about what kind of week you had and laughing and sharing a joke or something. But where the rubber really meets the road is on the Wednesday before Thanksgiving when you see people at headquarters going over [to the airport at Love Field], and even if they don't have the physical stamina to push wheelchairs or load baggage, they're taking cookies and brownies and cakes over there and wading through the throngs of passengers."

Owen explains that employees are not taking these treats to Southwest's passengers: The cookies and cakes represent support for their colleagues at Southwest who "are over there sweating bullets trying to get these massive amounts of people processed." This kind of support keeps Southwest one of the most productive companies in the history of the airline industry.

Organic Origins

Looking at Southwest Airlines from Owen's perspective, it is easy to see that the company's success comes from more than simple business practices. There is something more philosophical at work here. Owen says, "I do not think there is another company out there that has our culture and that has it in such an organic way."

Southwest's unique corporate culture was instilled from the outset. The reason why Southwest developed the culture it has today was simply a matter of survival in hostile Texas terrain. Since the roots of Southwest started to grow in an incredibly competitive environment, the company's culture played a large role in keeping the company—and its people—in the air during its first years of existence.

As described earlier, the company started in 1971 after three years of intense, expensive legal battles with two very entrenched Texas-based, incumbent carriers—Braniff and Texas Air—that did not want to see little Southwest Airlines get off the ground. "When these original employees back in '71 were coming to work every day," Owen says, "they had to rely on each other for this kind of support, because they didn't know if the next day they were going to have a job or if their checks were going to bounce. That's where a lot of this sense of humor and quirkiness came in. 'Hey, laugh today because we may all die tomorrow.'"

He continues: "I know a number of 'Originals,' and they all say that. They're like, 'Oh yeah. We did whatever we had to do to make sure it worked.' Then, over the years, as we became more and more successful, that became kind of a real underpinning of the way we were successful."

Helping Hands

Southwest has thrown many challenges to its employees throughout its existence as an airline. For example, the company faced an enormous challenge when United Airlines started its Shuttle by United service in California during the late 1980s. Shuttle by United was a new low-cost subsidiary operation of United Airlines that flew customers between San Francisco and Los Angeles.

To help the company compete against this new low-cost upstart and stay successful against a competitor with very deep pockets, Southwest asked its employees to contribute even more of their time. In return, Southwest poured support behind its people on the West Coast. One program was called "Helping Hands." Everybody in the company was encouraged to work in the field for a weekend to help out their coworkers.

Owen recalls, "We challenged our California employees unmercifully, and the way we challenged them is we dumped flights on them like you wouldn't believe. And we got them so far behind the learning curve, they couldn't hire people and train them fast enough. So they were having to do double and triple shifts to make it work. And we supported them by going out there and helping pack bags and cooking burgers for them and ordering pizza and saying, 'Hey, we know we're giving you an impossible challenge here, but thanks for doing it as well as you're doing it.'"

The camaraderie among coworkers at that time shifted from what Owen describes as "a type of gallows humor" to a real sense of support and pulling together so their company could extend its success from coast to coast. Owen remembers being one of the people who flew out to California to help his coworkers get through a difficult time: "People that were not working the field were absolutely encouraged to go out there and work. I very clearly remember working at LAX one Sunday morning and I was standing there tagging bags at the ticket counter with [then–chief financial officer] Gary Kelly, who is now our CEO, president, and chairman. And we looked up, and I don't think either one of us realized the amount of cruise traffic that comes through LAX. Well, apparently a dozen or so cruise ships had just docked at the Port of Long Beach, and we looked up and the lines were around our ticket counter, out the door, and all the way into Terminal 2. And I remember Gary going, 'Oh my God!'

"One of the supervisors who was working with us leaned over and said, 'Write checks, Gary. Write lots of checks.'"

In other words, the supervisor at the airport was encouraging his company's CFO to put more money into the airport's facilities so the company could handle such giant onslaughts of customers. As a result of Southwest's undaunted efforts to face its new competitor head on, the Shuttle by United regional airline was discontinued by United Airlines in 1991.

During Helping Hands and other such initiatives at Southwest, employees were not given extra days off for volunteering to help coworkers in the field, but the airline did pay for their hotel expenses and meals for the time they were helping their fellow employees. "You'd leave on a Friday afternoon, you'd go work your butt off Saturday and Sunday, and you'd fly home Sunday night so you were there at work on Monday morning," recalls Owen.

Since Southwest's employees receive free standby flights as part of their benefits package, those who went out into the field were able to fly for free. This meant that they were often getting the last seat on a plane or flying in the spare "jump seat" reserved for flight attendants.

Since there are four jump seats and usually only three flight attendants per flight, this seat can be used by a Southwest employee who is flying out to a field location to help his or her coworkers. But there is a catch to using the fourth jump seat: If you use it, you will probably be recruited by the flight crew to help out on the flight.

"I remember on a number of these, you'd get home Sunday night, and you're absolutely beat down, dead tired exhausted, but you'd feel so good about what you'd done, that there certainly wasn't complaining," Owen remembers. As part of the Helping Hands program, there were a limited number of assignments each weekend that Southwest employees could take to help their coworkers in the field. The program was so popular among Southwest employees that the company actually had to turn many volunteers away. "Altruism does exist," Owen declares.

Altruism

It seems that Southwest, through its programs that allow its employees to volunteer to work merely for the pleasure of helping their fellow coworkers, has tapped into some of the deeper functions of the brain that are only now just beginning to come to light through new neuroscience research. For example, recent studies of the human brain reveal that altruism is a wonderful motivator and can often be more powerful for driving behavior than monetary rewards.

In his book *How We Decide*, science writer Jonah Lehrer explains: "But here's a lovely secret of altruism: *it feels good*. The brain is designed so that acts of charity are pleasurable; being nice to others makes us feel nice."[9]

Lehrer goes on to describe a recent brain-imaging experiment involving a few dozen people. Each person was given $128. They were all allowed to either keep the money for themselves or donate the money to charity. Lehrer writes:

> When they chose to give away the money, the reward centers of their brains became active and they experienced the delightful glow of unselfishness. In fact, several subjects showed more reward-related brain activity during acts of altruism than they did when they actually received cash rewards. From the perspective of the brain, it literally was better to give than to receive.[10]

By tapping into the altruistic centers of the brains of its employees by creating voluntary work programs, Southwest is able not just to help its employees in the field get their work done but also to help the volunteers feel better about themselves and their jobs. It seems that science is only just beginning to prove what Southwest has known all along about the Golden Rule: Treating others as you want to be treated is not only good for business, it is good for everyone involved.

Executive Reciprocation

Owen has learned from many years of experience that his company's top officers understand the Golden Rule. He has seen them time and again step out from behind their desks to work side by side with their frontline employees to help them do their jobs. He has also experienced firsthand the ways executives and employees take care of each other in other ways. "We've been on Culture Committee trips with them where we're out standing on the ramp in Phoenix in August when it's 130 degrees, cooking hamburgers. We've been to family funerals in their family, or they've been to family funerals for our family."

This kind of camaraderie from the company's top officers helps Southwest's employees feel connected to their company and more secure about its future. Owen says, "It does inspire a whole lot more confidence, when you know somebody, and you know their heart like that. You know that they are good, giving, caring people. It's like that now. It was like that with Herb [Kelleher], and certainly with Colleen [Barrett]. You get to know them on that level."

NUTS ABOUT SOUTHWEST

While working on the Culture Committee, Bill Owen was able to learn much from Southwest's president emeritus Colleen Barrett, who has been with the company from its earliest days. Owen says that he has had even more contact with Barrett since the company started its Web log, *Nuts About Southwest* (www.blogsouthwest.com), two years ago.

As a regular contributor to Southwest's blog, Owen says he and his fellow company bloggers have been able to open up a whole new level of connection to people inside and outside the company. Sometimes their posts on that blog are strictly professional. Other times they are completely personal. But the end result is a feeling that Southwest cares about people and all of the things that make them people. "We were kind of given special dispensation to put as much of your heart and soul out there as you can," explains Owen. "And I have."

As a result, Owen has received many pieces of feedback from both Herb Kelleher and Barrett. "I had one blog piece," Owen recalls. "It's about a squirrel that showed up one morning in my commode. I won't go any further, but I got a call from Colleen. She said, 'Thanks! I just laughed so hard I peed thanks to you!'"

Transparency

Before any other airline had its own corporate blog, Southwest's product development manager, Angela Vargo, who worked in the company's Public Relations Department, had the idea for a Southwest blog back in 2005. She was interested in the emerging media at the time, and she saw the potential of a company blog. Vargo understood that blogging offers companies that are willing to embrace it an excellent way to become more transparent about their operations.

Two years later, in March 2007, *Nuts About Southwest* went online. It started with a core group of bloggers who were each handpicked by Barrett. Those first bloggers were picked, according to Owen, "because she knew our writing styles and she knew us well enough to know our hearts, so we wouldn't embarrass her."

Blogging at Southwest also offers the company a way to share pertinent information with whoever is interested in reading about what is going on inside the company. Whether they are customers, competitors, shareholders, employees, or executives, everyone can learn more about what the company is doing and how each person fits into what is going on.

Public Relations and the Web Log

While the company still has a Public Relations Department that issues press releases and makes announcements to the media about its activities, Southwest's Web log supplements that type of formal information with a more informal look at the company's news, people, and events. As Owen notes, Southwest Airlines is more than a company made up of airplanes: "We're a company of 35,000 people, and we all have our stories. While we have our work stories, we also have our stories about our lives."

Owen says that blogging allows Southwest's people to describe their work and the company's news in a much more personal voice. This helps readers get more excited about the information than a standard press release, and this helps to draw them in. "It really does just bring a brand new level of transparency to the company's communication efforts."

The Personal Edge

Another effect of Southwest's corporate blog that nobody foresaw is the way mainstream media embrace the information that is being posted there. The blog at Southwest and other corporate blogs have now become standard media outlets that reporters go to for story ideas and quotes about news going on inside a company. "They'll quote the blog without ever calling to fact-check with Public Relations because it's developed that kind of credibility with them," Owen explains. Plus, the blog contains the personal edge that every reporter is looking for when writing a good news story.

Southwest has learned that it can combine the homespun stories of squirrels in commodes, recipes for favorite desserts, and the more polished stories about customer initiatives to create a portal that can serve all of its stakeholders' needs, as well as the media's need for accurate news about the company. Although his story about the squirrel was not picked up by any mainstream media outlets, Owen points out that it was carried on about fifteen to twenty other blogs on the Internet.

Flight Numbering

One blog post that Owen wrote which received much more attention from the public was his story about flight numbers. As lead planner in Southwest's Planning Department, he has the inside scoop on the numbers that go along with the flights that his company flies each day. To help customers decode some of the mystery in the numbering of flights, he published his insights on Southwest's corporate blog on May 9, 2006. Under the title "'Flight Names' Just Wouldn't Be the Same," he revealed the secrets behind the art of numbering flights for Southwest. That post was then linked to by a number of other popular air travel blogs in the blogosphere, including FlyerTalk.com, Airliners.net, and Crankyflier.com.

As Owen tells it: "In the piece, I went through some of the history of flight numbers, like every airline's 'Flight 1' tends to be their premier flight. Our Flight 1 is our 7 o'clock from Dallas to Houston. It's the first flight we ever flew. American Airlines' Flight 1 is JFK [in New York City] to LAX [Los Angeles]: American's flagship service. At the old PanAm, God rest its soul, Flight 1 was the around-the-world flight that went JFK to Los Angeles to Honolulu to Tokyo to Hong Kong to New Delhi and on around the world."

In his piece, Owen points out that some airlines will number their flights from east to west with odd numbers, and those from west to east with even numbers, but he explains that Southwest doesn't do this because its route network is so dense that they could not get that type of system to work efficiently. He adds, "One time, when I added a whole bunch of service to Vegas just on the weekends, I made it so every flight number that I used for that new service to and from Vegas, if you added up all the numbers of the flight number, they added up to twenty-one. Our flight 711 goes to Vegas."

Owen says that an airline's flight 1776 will usually go to Philadelphia. Similarly, flights to Columbus, Ohio, are often designated 1492. "There is some humor involved in flight numbers," he concludes.

THE WORK ENVIRONMENT

Humor at Work

The idea of humor comes up again and again when talking with the people at Southwest Airlines. While humor helps employees cope with some of the more tedious tasks of their jobs, such as numbering thousands of flights every day throughout the company's system, it also helps to attract customers and employees to the company.

When asked how Southwest infuses humor throughout its operations, Bill Owen says, "You hire for it. From the outset, you hire people that seem to have the right attitude and that seem like they know how to have a good time. They don't have to be stand-up comedians, but as long as you've got people that aren't afraid to laugh at themselves as well as laugh at other things, then you've probably got a good foundation."

When Owen worked at American Airlines, on the Wednesday before the last Thanksgiving he worked there, he suggested to his co-workers that they bake cookies and take them over to the airport to show their support for the people who had to work on the front lines on one of the busiest travel days of the year. He recalls, "Everybody just kind of looked at me and said, 'You are so weird. No. We're going to be getting ready for our family Thanksgiving.' If you did that at Southwest, the only fight that you'd have break out is who's going to make chocolate chip and who's going to make peanut butter. It's just that kind of place."

A bird's eye view of the interior of Southwest's headquarters at Dallas Love Field. (Courtesy Southwest Airlines.)

Giving employees the freedom to have a good time at work is part of the corporate culture at Southwest. At the company's headquarters, coworkers constantly play harmless practical jokes on each other throughout the day. Owen explains, "You almost budget your time so you can budget fun in your work day."

"A Sense of Family"

Through humor and other positive personal interactions, people connect with each other like family members. Southwest's leaders nurture these connections by instilling their policies with a sense of love and a sense of freedom. They also model the behaviors they want to see among their employees.

In *The Service Profit Chain,* a book written while Herb Kelleher was still CEO of Southwest, coauthors James L. Heskett, W. Earl Sasser Jr., and Leonard A. Schlesinger write:

> Herb Kelleher will tell you that his most important task is insuring that the organization remembers these two important sources of focus: high value service to customers who appreciate what that means at Southwest Airlines and the preservation of a sense of family in the company's organization.[11]

Emotions

The emotional content of the interactions among coworkers at Southwest is not missed by the authors of *The Service Profit Chain.* They observe:

> Hugging is a serious activity among employees at Southwest. A casual walk between offices at headquarters becomes an extended exercise in getting caught up on business and personal affairs. It slowly dawns on a visitor that these people aren't putting on an act; they really like each other. It may explain why they are able to work approximately 20 percent more productively than employees of other airlines for about the same amount of pay, which in turn explains why Southwest is able to deliver such high value to its customers.[12]

Hugs are free, but, as Southwest proves by its business success, the productivity hugs can create when they are part of an employee culture that promotes human expressions of kindness and gratitude can be an underlying source of great financial rewards.

Diversity

At Southwest, allowing people to be themselves goes beyond simply letting people express their sense of humor on the job. As a demonstration of its belief that people should be able to be themselves, it has also adopted numerous people-friendly policies that have brought the company accolades from many organizations that monitor how well companies treat their people on a variety of issues. For example, in September 2009, Southwest scored an "outstanding" 95 out of 100 on the Corporate Equality Index of the Human Rights Campaign (HRC), which means that Southwest is recognized as a "green" company that receives the support of the HRC. The Corporate Equality Index is a tool that measures how equitably companies are treating their gay, lesbian, bisexual, and transgender employees, consumers, and investors. The HRC encourages consumers to make every effort to support businesses rated as green (i.e., those receiving a rating between 80 and 100).

In its policy on harassment and discrimination, signed by CEO Gary Kelly and posted on its Web site, Southwest states that the company prohibits any kind of harassment and discrimination against its employees by people inside or outside of the company. It specifies:

> Harassment or discrimination based on race, color, religion, age, sex, sexual orientation, gender identity, pregnancy, marital status, national origin, disability, veteran status, or other protected status, negatively affects morale, motivation, and job performance. Such behavior is inappropriate, offensive, and will not be tolerated; and it is contrary to the Southwest Spirit and the Southwest Culture.[13]

Diversity is important to Southwest Airlines. To demonstrate this to its employees, customers, and shareholders, and to reap the many benefits of a diversity of opinions in the workplace, Southwest has a Diversity Council that meets six times a year to discuss and support a variety of diversity efforts within the company. These include recruiting and advancing women and minorities, educating employees regarding diversity awareness, and increasing supplier diversity. The company's Diversity Council also helps Southwest improve diversity and inclusiveness within the company.

Southwest Airlines also has a Supplier Diversity Program, which supports suppliers that share Southwest's ideals. Its policy for suppliers states, "As a Company, Southwest Airlines Co. values diversity and seeks to create an environment that encourages it, both in the workplace and among our supplier base."[14]

Ethical Business

In 2007, *Business Ethics,* the magazine of corporate responsibility, ranked Southwest Airlines thirty-third on its "100 Best Corporate Citizens" list. In 2002, *Business Ethics* also honored the company by placing it on the list in the number 20 spot. In the accompanying magazine article, writer Mary Miller wrote that Southwest was one of four firms that tied for the magazine's top score for "service to employees":

> What's striking about this firm is its no-layoff policy. In the wake of the Sept. 11 terrorist attack when the industry faced significant losses, many airlines cut schedules and reduced workforces by up to 20 percent. Southwest did not lay off employees then, nor has it ever in its 31-year history.[15]

In Miller's article, Southwest spokesperson Linda Rutherford explains that the company survived the 9/11 crisis thanks to the employees' keen focus on keeping the company a low-cost operation, along with the support employees received from upper management in the form of a well-communicated plan for making it through a challenging time. Rutherford added, "There's a lot of psychic value in that. It created a sense of stability that allowed our employee team to focus more quickly."[16] Dedication to its employees, stability, and focus are three ways Southwest keeps its people engaged and its customers enamored.

REDUCED FUEL CONSUMPTION

Southwest's interest in preserving the environment goes beyond serving its coffee in cups made from recycled paper (which it does). One way the company demonstrates its leaders' interest in environmentally sound business practices is its efforts to reduce fuel consumption and greenhouse gas emissions through investments in the Required Navigations Performances (RNP) project.

An *eTurbo News* story quoted Southwest Airlines Executive Vice President and Chief of Operations Mike Van de Ven as saying, "RNP allows the aircraft to fly more precise, direct, and accurate paths, allowing more 'lanes' to be built into the same limited airspace." The article continues:

> In support of the FAA's Roadmap for Performance-Based Navigation, Southwest has made a commitment to invest $175 million over the next six years to implement RNP procedures at all 64 airports the airline serves. The initial investment will provide long-term benefits to industry congestion and aircraft efficiencies. For a single minute of time saved on each flight, the

annual savings quickly add up to 156,000 metric tons of reduction in emissions per year (by 2015), and $25 million in fuel savings per year.[17]

By putting its corporate practices where its sustainability statement is, Southwest saves money while saving the planet for future generations.

MARK TWAIN

While Southwest Airlines serves as a corporate role model for other organizations, showing them how to add love and freedom to their work, improve diversity, increase sustainability, act ethically, and protect the environment by reducing greenhouse gas emissions, it also does something else that is changing the world in many wonderful ways. It is bringing people around the world together and improving their relationships by demonstrating how a low-fare airline business model can succeed.

In 1896, Mark Twain wrote:

Travel is fatal to prejudice, bigotry, and narrow-mindedness, and many of our people need it sorely on these accounts. Broad, wholesome, charitable views of men and things cannot be acquired by vegetating in one little corner of the earth all one's lifetime.[18]

By allowing more people to travel through increased accessibility and lower-cost flights, and by showing airlines in other countries how to do the same, Southwest is helping to reduce prejudice around the country and the world.

Chapter Seven

Southwest's People and Planes

PERKS

When employees join Southwest, they are eligible for unlimited free flights for themselves, their parents, their children, and their spouses. Their children can fly for free on Southwest until they are age eighteen or, if they go to college, age twenty-three. This free-flight benefit starts on the first day the employee starts to work for Southwest Airlines.

All of these people fly standby, which means that they are limited by the space available on the plane. If the aircraft reaches capacity of paying customers, employees get bumped to the next flight. The company also allows what they call "committed/registered partners" to fly for free as well, but they must pay the cost of taxes.

Southwest's senior director of culture services, Sunny Abercrombie, says that having this flight benefit "is awesome. The flights really do keep a lot of people here." She explains that many people who work in the company's Dallas headquarters come in at an entry level, but stay with the company because the health benefits and the flight benefits are so good.

Other perks enjoyed by employees include the ability to earn what Southwest calls "Buddy Passes." This Buddy Pass program allows employees to earn up to four passes each quarter, depending on the hours they work, that they can share with anyone, including friends and family members who are not covered by their flight benefits. Employees also receive discounted fares at many other airlines, thanks to reciprocal agreements that the company has within the industry. This internal travel agency group is called the Southwest Airlines Pass Bureau. The company also has discount agreements with several rental car companies, hotels, and theme parks that also benefit employees when they travel. All of these perks help to keep Southwest's employees motivated, productive, and long-term.

LEADERSHIP AT THE TOP

Although Colleen Barrett has officially retired from her role as Southwest president, she continues to remain an employee and receive a salary from the company as president emeritus. In this role, she continues to put the same love and care into Southwest's employees and customers that she did when she helped to run the company.

Today, Barrett is still a member of the Culture Committee she once created. She also helps to guide the employees and leaders at Southwest, ensuring that they are happy and productive in their roles. Abercrombie says that Barrett "sees potential and seizes it. She has an uncanny way of finding out if you're in the right job or not. She may think an employee is doing a really good job, but she has this uncanny way of knowing, 'Are you really where you are supposed to be, or wouldn't you be better doing this?' She has a lot of influence on a lot of our employees. A lot of our officers are where they are today because of her."

Barrett makes it her business to know the employees' business. As president emeritus, she still maintains incredible influence over Southwest's employee culture and continues to help it succeed through her active participation and support. Abercrombie says that, although "President Emeritus" is on Barrett's letterhead today, she would prefer to be considered a "Southwest employee." While Abercrombie continues to call Barrett "Colleen" when they work together, she admits that sometimes, like other employees, she calls her "Mama" as well.

Today, Herb Kelleher is chairman emeritus. Like Barrett, he also likes to be called by a more informal name by Southwest's employees, so they call him "Herb." Abercrombie says, "I've heard people refer to them as 'Mrs. Barrett' or 'Mr. Kelleher,' and they're both like, 'No. Call me Colleen,' or 'Call me Herb.'"

Herb Kelleher's Laugh

Kelleher's reputation as a fun-loving person and leader is confirmed time and again by Southwest's employees. "He is probably the one person in the world that makes me laugh more than anybody," says Abercrombie. "And he can make me laugh just by hearing him laugh. He has unbelievable, just crazy, one-of-a-kind laughs."

While Kelleher was CEO and Barrett was president of Southwest Airlines, Abercrombie's office was located in the company's Dallas headquarters next door to their offices. She says that even on her worst days at work, the sound of Kelleher's laugh would remind her why Southwest Airlines is such a wonderful place to work. She says, "He's such an amazing person."

One of Kelleher's personality traits that sets him apart from most other people is his ability to remember the names of people he meets for the first time. According to Abercrombie, "He may not see them for six or seven more months, and he'll walk up to them and know them by name. And that is just one of the things that's so amazing about him, and one of the things that endears him so much to our employees."

"The Most Important Person in the Room"

Abercrombie observes that Kelleher's ability to focus only on the single person he is talking to also makes him a beloved figure among Southwest's employees. "It could be me, President Obama, and Chuck Yeager, for example, and if he were already talking to me when they walked in the room, his eyes would stay focused on me until he finished the story he was telling or finished the conversation he was having with me before he would turn and look at the more important people. He's always been that way, and that's just what makes people feel so good around him, and so important around him. It could be anybody. It could be somebody from the mailroom that he's talking to, but he will finish that conversation and make you feel like you're the most important person in that room."

Abercrombie says that it feels good going to work every day knowing that she is employed by people who hold and perpetuate these kinds of positive values and act as living examples of strong, ethical principles all the time. She says, "For me, I'll tell you, that's why I'm still here."

Knowing that she could work anywhere in the world that she wants, Abercrombie says she stays at Southwest because she wants to continue to work for people she believes in. Southwest hires the kinds of people she wants to be around. These are the people who have become her best friends. "I have lots of friends outside the company, but some of my very best friends are here," Abercrombie adds.

Gary Kelly

Abercrombie and current Southwest CEO Gary Kelly were both hired to work for Southwest in 1986, and both began working for the airline in its finance department. She has watched him move up the ranks from chief financial officer to chief executive officer to chairman of the company, and she says he has not changed as a person. And, over the years, she says he has continued to support Southwest's unique corporate culture from every position he has held.

"He's really been a champion for our culture all along," Abercrombie points out. "And he's one of the ones who has really understood it and really knows what it means, and how incredibly important it is for our survival and moving forward."

Kelly has proven this in many ways. For example, he was the executive who approved the Culture Ambassadors program. Those eight ambassadors would not be out in the field if it weren't for his signature and support. Kelly is also an important champion behind Southwest's "Own the Holidays" effort. In addition, as a protégé of Kelleher and Barrett, he has continued to enthusiastically support all of the work done by Culture Services.

The State of Our Airline Address

Another of Southwest's annual activities that is coordinated by the Culture Activities team is a program called "Messages to the Field." As part of this program, the team takes Kelly out to six of Southwest's largest markets, where he delivers a message to the employees in each of those cities, much like the U.S. president's State of the Union Address. Kelly's speech is called the State of Our Airline Address. This is an event that began when Kelleher was CEO of the airline and continued under Jim Parker when he succeeded Kelleher as CEO. Today, Kelly keeps the tradition alive.

During the addresses, which take place in February of each year, Kelly describes the major issues and challenges faced by the airline in the previous year as well as the direction the company wants to go over the current year. As he tells company employees about the current state of the industry, he puts Southwest into that context and shows how the company stands among its competitors. The event comes across as a pep rally for Southwest's employees, who celebrate the event as an exciting occasion.

In previous years, Kelleher would often be the center of jokes at these occasions, which created a fun atmosphere. Following in his footsteps, Kelly is not afraid to poke fun at himself at these events either. For example, 2009's events had a rock star theme. Kelly, who plays the electric guitar, performed with a live band in front of the cheering crowds of employees. The song he played, called "Southwest Warriors," was written especially for the Messages to the Field program.

Earning Employee Respect

Abercrombie says this year's events were a terrific success because of Kelly's great attitude: "He understands that he's never going to be exactly like Herb, but he also understands that he can't take himself too seriously. He has a very serious job, but he has to have fun with it. And he's doing a great job of that. I think he's earned a lot of respect from our employees."

Kelly also shows his leadership capabilities by staying focused on the things that have made Southwest so successful over the past four decades. By keeping many of the big events alive during the economic recession of 2009—for example, refusing to cancel Southwest's annual awards banquet—he bucked his critics and showed Southwest's employees that he values their service to the company. He understands that employees worked just as hard, if not harder, in 2009 than employees in the past, so they deserved to be rewarded just as much as those employees in the past who were honored with a yearly ceremony for their contributions to the company. His support of the banquet was just one way that he showed Southwest's employees that they are the backbone of the company's success.

Abercrombie explains this by looking at Southwest's cultural values. "We're a family at Southwest," she says. "When you're having tough times at home, you don't cancel birthdays or you don't cancel Christmas. You celebrate them. You just might not do as much as you normally would."

Southwest did, in fact, spend less on 2009's awards banquet, but it made sure that none of the cutbacks would be noticeable to the employees who attended. Abercrombie says the team that put on the event just worked a little harder behind the scenes to make it a success than they had to in past years. She adds that it wouldn't have been possible without Kelly's support: "I think he's doing a fantastic job. I really do."

BUYOUT PACKAGES

As described earlier, even in tough economic times, Southwest has never laid off any of its employees. Instead, Southwest has been able to trim some of its expenses by offering buyout packages to any employees who might be thinking about leaving the company for whatever reason. The most recent of these came in early 2009. Southwest's buyout was offered to all employees below the director level, based on years of service to the company. An office administrator in each department was available to counsel employees about making that choice.

Although she has worked for the company for twenty-three years, Sunny Abercrombie says she's not ready to leave the job she loves. She explains, "I figure if there ever comes a time when I stop loving what I do, then that really is the time to give somebody else a chance. But I'm just not there yet."

CHARITABLE GIVING

Another aspect of Southwest Airlines that makes it very different from other airlines is its deep charitable giving. Southwest's employees have always rallied around a cause. Since the beginning of the company, if an employee has suffered a catastrophic event such as a death in the family or a debilitating injury, the hat will come out and people will donate what they can to help that person get through his or her time of need.

Southwest Airlines Employees Catastrophic Assistance Charity

Back in 1990, Southwest employee Randy Rickard, who has since retired, had the idea to start a more formal assistance program for employees in times of need. He spearheaded a program through which Southwest employees could help each other by donating a small amount from each of their paychecks. The program became the Southwest Airlines Employees Catastrophic Assistance Charity (ECAC). With the funds collected, employees help other employees who suffer a serious setback such as a medical emergency or an unexpected financial hardship.

To distribute the money, an ECAC board of directors was established. This board meets every two weeks to review applications that are sent to the fund. While the fund's primary source of income is the money deducted from employee paychecks, it also receives money from company fundraisers, speaker fees earned when company officers and employees participate in speaking engagements, leftover department "party funds," employee golf tournaments, and private donations. All of the money donated to this certified charity is tax deductible. As a certified charity, auditors from the Internal Revenue Service review its books to make sure everything is run correctly.

In a recent interview with Steve Heaser, the host of Southwest's "Redbelly Radio" podcast, Rickard described the origins of the ECAC:

> It started as a result of our desire to be able to help employees in a real measurable way if something happened to them. Up to that point in time, people could only pass the hat in their local environment and raise perhaps a couple hundred dollars or so, but that might not fill a need. So, we thought that if every employee contributed a very small amount, that amount magnified by the number of employees, if somebody had a problem, there would be sufficient funds—and a pot to go to—to really help them out.[1]

While Southwest's insurance benefit is usually sufficient to cover employees' medical costs, the fund is intended to help people who are struck with unexpected costs that insurance does not cover, such as a high deductible or emergency child care.

All of the donations made to the 501(c)(3) charity go directly to employees. Rickard explains:

> All of our contributions, 100 percent, pass down to our employees. There are no basic overhead costs other than clerical costs,

and that's covered by the dividends and the interest we get on the investment. So, the actual money that an employee contributes, 100 percent goes to other employees.

As a result of the success of this first-of-its-kind program, other companies, such as Boeing, have come to Southwest to learn how to establish internal charity programs of their own.

In May 2009, the ECAC crossed an amazing milestone: The fund had given away a total of more than $10 million in gifts to Southwest's employees in need over the nineteen years of its existence. In the beginning, the fund collected only 25 or 50 cents per employee paycheck, which did not add up to much in its early years. For this reason, the $10 million landmark is particularly remarkable. Rickard says, "To have this amount of money in this relatively short period of time given out to Southwest employees is really an incredible reflection on how well the Southwest employees care about each other." Today, some employees donate $1, $20, or even $50 per paycheck.

By showing its people how to care for others with people-centric actions, Southwest's founders demonstrated role-model behaviors that Rickard took to heart. He then put the ethical values they displayed into action in a new, innovative way. The meaningful giving that is embodied by the work done by the ECAC fund is yet another example of the way that Southwest Airlines and its people put people first.

Hurricane Katrina

When a large catastrophic event takes place where many people in a specific region are affected, such as Hurricane Katrina in 2005, a fund like the ECAC can be a much better way to serve the large numbers of people who are in need at the same time. Rickard points out that passing the hat could not have met the demands of the people in New Orleans who were affected by Katrina as efficiently as the fund that he had helped to establish nineteen years ago: "The best way to do it is to have everybody give a little bit, which doesn't hurt them. That little bit builds up over time, and when something like that happens, then we can help in a very meaningful way."

Sunny Abercrombie joined the Southwest Airlines ECAC review board in 1992. She recalls, "When Katrina hit, we had our command center set up for our operation, but also, within that room, there was an area set up just for us so we could go in. As soon as they started locating those employees, we were like, 'What do you need? Are you in a hotel? Do you have cash? Did you lose everything?' We were able to get funds either transferred out of our account straight into theirs or get a Visa gift card to send out right away for them so they could go get a hotel, go get a meal, go replace the clothing they lost."

Extra Help in an Emergency

Any time there is an emergency where Southwest's employees need extra help, such as Hurricane Ike in 2008 or a catastrophic fire, the Southwest Airlines ECAC fund's board works hard to get money to the people who need it. If there is a large emergency between board meetings, the board will get together as soon as possible to get help to those in need. Abercrombie explains: "During a hurricane, if an employee's got six kids, we're going to give them enough money to feed and clothe six kids plus themselves. The same would be [true] if it's an illness. A lot of times, people have a sick child, and they just can't get ahead of the medical bills, or the time they need to take off to be with them. They don't have accrued time or vacation time, so we'll help them with their salary. Sometimes we even pay their COBRA [extended health] benefits. If that's the best thing for them to keep them insured as they go through their treatment, then that's what we'll do."

GROWING UP WITH SOUTHWEST

Abercrombie says the people at Southwest Airlines are like a family with whom she has grown up: "I really grew up here. I came to work here when I was young and a little wild." She says that she didn't have a clue about what she wanted to do with her life until she was hired by Southwest. "I felt this incredible sense of family and belonging. And then, of course, I had Colleen [Barrett] to raise me."

She explains that her experiences with Southwest have taught her much about the airline industry, but she has also learned a great deal about people and serving others. She has learned to respect the differences of people, whether those differences are generational, regional, or ethnic. "People are different wherever you go, but basically they're all the same. And they want one thing: They want to be appreciated. And they want to know that they're appreciated. They want you to tell them."

Abercrombie believes that this lesson has helped her grow as a Southwest employee, but it has also helped her in her personal life as well. She says that she was once much more self-centered in her personal life. She also used to believe that physical possessions were much more important. But today, her experiences at Southwest have changed her outlook on life. Instead of buying her nephews expensive gifts for their birthdays, Abercrombie has learned that a phone call is even more appreciated and personal. Her work at Southwest has made her much more patient with other people. "I realized that my time is valuable to me, but their time should also be valuable to me because I don't know how much time I'm going to have with them." She adds, "I've just grown up a lot."

HARDWARE

While Southwest's dedicated people make up its foundation of quality service, the company has made a name for itself among its competitors, employees, and customers with more than its unique hiring practices and groundbreaking corporate culture. Another aspect of the company that has made it very different from the other carriers that came before it is the strategy it used when choosing its aircraft. With only a couple of short-term exceptions, the airline has only ever flown Boeing 737s. As Southwest President Colleen Barrett noted in 2002, "Southwest Airlines has built its reputation on low fares and quality service throughout the United States, and we continue to see a bright future by utilizing an all-737 fleet." This decision not only has made Southwest Airlines a highly profitable company but also changed the way other airlines around the world do business.

The Boeing 737

The Boeing 737 is the most popular airliner in the world. According to Boeing, "the entire 737 family has won orders for more than 8,000 airplanes." This is more airplanes than Boeing's biggest competitor has sold for its entire product line. "No other jet airplane in commercial aviation history has achieved the sales success of the 737," Boeing boasts. "The 737—a short-to-medium-range airplane—is based on a key Boeing philosophy of delivering added value to airlines with reliability, simplicity, and reduced operating and maintenance costs."[2]

Reliability

The reason Southwest has chosen the Boeing 737 as its aircraft of choice is the 737's reputation for reliability. The airplane is easier for pilots to quickly turn around at the gate than larger commercial aircraft, which allows Southwest Airlines to stay on schedule and satisfy customer expectations for timely flights. These attributes help Southwest create value for its passengers.

On average, Southwest flies 6.2 flights each day on each of its aircraft—roughly 12 hours and 9 minutes per day.

Toby Bright, executive vice president of sales at Boeing Commercial Airplanes, notes, "The 737's reliability also means operators can use an airline for more flights on any given day, giving passengers more departure time choices and airlines the opportunities for more revenue."[3] The Boeing 737 is Southwest Airlines' secret weapon against higher fares. By tapping into this source of cost savings and faster flight turn times, Southwest not only saves money for itself but has also shown other airlines across the globe how to do the same.

In 2002, the Boeing 737 made up more than 90 percent of the combined fleets of all of the low-fare airlines around the globe. The profitability of these carriers is closely tied to the cost savings that the Boeing 737 offers, thanks to the aircraft's reliability, low maintenance costs, and low operating costs. Carriers that follow Southwest's model of using only 737s include WestJet, Ryanair, GOL, and Virgin Blue. In 2002, the European airline BMI started its own exclusively Boeing 737 low-fare carrier, BMI Baby, which had nine of the aircraft by 2007.

The Southwest Fleet

As of 2009, Southwest Airlines had 181 Boeing 737-300s, which seat 137 passengers; 25 Boeing 737-500s, which seat 122; and 338 Boeing 737-700s, which seat 137. Southwest's fleet has an average age of approximately ten years.

Boeing rolled out its first 737-300 on January 17, 1984, and its first flight was on February 24 that year. After 1,300 flight-test hours, the 737-300 was certified by the FAA. Southwest and USAir were the first launch customers for the Boeing 737-300.

The 737-500 made its maiden flight on June 30, 1989. According to *The Vital Guide to Commercial Aircraft and Airliners*:

> The 737-500 measures 101 ft. 9 in. (31 m), almost exactly the same size as the 737-200 [the 737-300 is 109 ft. 7 in. (33.4 m) long]. By mid-1994, deliveries for the 737-300/400 ($27–31 million) stood at 1,227, and at 277 for the 737-500 ($26 million).
>
> In November 1993, Southwest Airlines launched the next chapter in the 737 story with an order for 63 Boeing 737-Xs, with another 63 on option. . . . Southwest has ordered the 110-ft. 2-in. (33.6-m) 737-700 (formerly 737-300X).[4]

On November 7, 1997, Boeing welcomed a new member of the 737 family: the Next-Generation 737-700.

All 737 models are powered by CFM56-7 engines produced by CFMI, a joint venture of General Electric of the United States and Snecma of France.

Advantages of the 737

The Boeing 737 offers airlines both range flexibility and interior flexibility. According to the salespeople at Boeing:

> Operators can choose optional flex seating, in which they can change a row of seats from five-abreast business-class seating to six-abreast tourist-class seating in less than one minute.

A moveable cabin divider also allows configuration changes between flights.[5]

Southwest started its operations in 1971 with three Boeing 737s in the 300 series. When the 500 series of 737s was launched, Southwest was the first customer to fly them. Then, in 1997, when Boeing manufactured its first 700-series 737s, Southwest was once again Boeing's launch customer for the new aircraft.

One customization of Southwest's airplanes is the performance-enhancing blended winglets that have been added to all of its fleet of 737-700s. Every new 737-700 that Southwest buys from Boeing arrives with these blended winglets already installed. In early 2007, Southwest started to retrofit all of its Boeing 737-300s with the winglets, and it planned to complete the project by the end of 2009.

STANDING OUT

Most of Southwest's airplanes are painted gold, red, orange, and blue. While these aircraft stand out among other airplanes, there are many other airplanes in Southwest's fleet that get even more attention from those who see them in the sky or on the runway:

- Three of Southwest's 737s look like Shamu, SeaWorld's famous killer whale.
- One airplane, christened *Lone Star One*, is painted like the Texas flag to celebrate Southwest's twentieth anniversary in 1991.
- *Silver One* is decorated in honor of the company's twenty-fifth anniversary.
- Another airplane, *Arizona One*, celebrates that state's importance to Southwest's history.
- *California One* similarly pays tribute to that state's heritage. Other state-dedicated planes include *New Mexico One*, *Nevada One*, *Maryland One*, and *Illinois One*.

Another uniquely decorated aircraft in Southwest's fleet is *Triple Crown One*, which honors Southwest's employees for winning five consecutive airline Triple Crown awards, which are bestowed for the best service in three categories: best on-time record, best baggage handling, and fewest complaints from customers. The overhead bins inside *Triple Crown One* are inscribed with the names of all of the people who were working for Southwest Airlines at the time that the fifth award was given to the company.

After the National Basketball Association honored Southwest by making it the professional basketball league's official airline, a 737 called the *Slam Dunk One* was created in 2005. The outside of this

In 1995, Southwest Airlines launched *California One* in Sacramento and tours it throughout the state. (Courtesy Southwest Airlines.)

737 is bright blue and orange, with a large basketball painted on the front of the plane. On the inside, a different NBA team logo is painted on each overhead bin.

These aircraft show Southwest's pride in the airline, its people, and their Boeing 737s. While he was still CEO, Herb Kelleher declared, "It's difficult for me to visualize Southwest Airlines without the 737. It's beautifully designed and manufactured, and I think one of the best decisions we ever made was to buy the Boeing 737."[6]

On November 4, 2005, Southwest Airlines launched the NBA-themed specialty airplane *Slam Dunk One* to celebrate its partnership with the National Basketball Association. (Courtesy Southwest Airlines.)

Chapter Eight

Hiring and Training: Southwest's University for People

JON SHUBERT

Hired by Southwest Airlines in January 1989, Jon Shubert is now a twenty-year veteran of the company. He joined Southwest as a telephone representative in the Customer Relations Department. At the time, Southwest had recently divided that department into two parts: telephone representatives and writers. Before that, Customer Relations employees did both duties, but in the late 1980s, the department found advantages in allowing its people to specialize in one of the two areas.

When Shubert was hired, he and two other people were put into the new Telephone Representative Division. Since Southwest prefers to hire from within, one of those people was a transfer from another department in its Dallas headquarters, but Shubert and the third person were brand new to the company and the airline industry.

With his English degree and some prior experience in customer relations, Southwest saw Shubert as a prime candidate for the challenges of this new role in the Customer Relations Department. Another thing that he had going for him was the fact that his wife had been working for the company for seven and a half years. (Today, Shubert's wife has been with the company for a total of twenty-eight years: twenty-three in reservations, and five as a telephone representative in the Customer Relations Department—the very same position into which Shubert was first hired.)

The Informal Interview

After an interview with the director of customer relations and Colleen Barrett, who was the executive in charge of the Customer Relations Department at the time, Shubert got the job. He says his interview at Southwest was unlike any interview he had ever experienced. It was much more informal and much less "official," stilted, and structured than those he had undergone with previous employers. It took place in

Barrett's office. The director of customer relations, Jim Rupple (who is now vice president of customer relations), was there, too.

Shubert recalls: "I went into her office and sat on a pretty big, overstuffed couch, and I just kind of fell back into it, kind of awkwardly, and straightened myself up, but it didn't seem to raise any eyebrows. They were just interested in talking with me as a person. The questions were not real structured. They were more interested in what attitude I could bring to the job than what my experiences in the past were."

He says his degree in English also played a part in his being hired because the new Customer Relations telephone representative position was designed to be a stepping-stone toward the writing position in the department. The two company leaders explained to him that once he got some experience on the telephone, he could then become eligible for the writer position.

Over the past twenty years, this thinking at Southwest has shifted a little. Now, the company realizes that some people are simply better on the phone, and others are better at writing, so today, Southwest Airlines acknowledges that those two skills are not always interchangeable, and the two roles are less intertwined. Nevertheless, at the time, Shubert saw the writing position as a future goal.

"The Right Kind of Attitude"

Shubert says that although he felt more comfortable than he had in past interviews at other companies, he was still somewhat uncomfortable for several reasons. "Not only were the top two folks there, but also it was kind of awkward for me because I wasn't expecting it to be so informal and unstructured." Shubert says the experience was very different than he had expected. "It wasn't what I would call a 'corporate' interview by the corporate interviewers or recruiters or HR people."

SOUTHWEST'S HIRING PROCESS

In an article for *Fortune Small Business*, Justin Martin wrote about how much small businesses can learn from companies such as Southwest Airlines, as well as General Electric and Dell. In the article, Martin explains that Southwest's personnel practices are what set it apart from its competitors. Focusing on the interview and hiring process, he quotes consultant and former Southwest employee Rita Bailey, who says that Southwest's people are the company's "secret weapon" for success.

While showing small company representatives how to capitalize on the business practices of Southwest Airlines, she points to the company's hiring methods as a groundbreaking process to emulate. Martin explains:

> When hiring, the company emphasizes attitude over skill. The thinking here: Skills can always be taught on the job, but attitude is pretty well hard-wired. As a result Southwest interviews are full of questions designed to suss out an applicant's personality, congeniality, style, and coping skills.[1]

Some interviewees say they've been asked questions such as, "If you were a tree, what kind of tree would you be?" Although there is no right or wrong answer, questions such as this allow interviewers to see their prospects work through their answers and hear how their sense of humor plays into the situation. A sense of humor is crucial to the successful candidate.

By identifying a sense of humor during job interviews, Southwest can better determine who will fit into Southwest's unique corporate culture, and those who will struggle with it. Those with a stronger sense of humor usually have a stronger sense of who they are and are more comfortable with themselves and the people with whom they work, including customers and fellow employees.

Bailey understands the rationale behind this way of thinking. In Martin's article, Bailey says, "If people don't have a sense of identity, then it becomes just a job."[2] Helping its people express their own identities by offering them the latitude to be themselves on the job is how Southwest builds morale and keeps its employees productive and happy.

Hiring for Attitude

When Southwest hires new employees, the company looks for more than skills. It is seeking the right personality for its company culture.

Herb Kelleher once said, "Hiring starts off looking for people with a good attitude—that's what we're looking for—people who enjoy serving other people."[3] Southwest employee Bill Owen can attest to the reality of Kelleher's words.

When Owen wanted to move up in the company and into the Schedule Planning Department, he was one of two candidates for a single job opening in the department. He explains that when his supervisors asked him to come in for a lunch interview, he brought cupcakes. But these were not ordinary cupcakes. Before baking them, Owen bought several pairs of plastic novelty nose-glasses, complete with Groucho Marx–style moustache and eyebrows. Then he cut them apart so he ended up with just the noses. "I made a batch of two dozen vanilla cupcakes," he recalls, "iced them with chocolate frosting, and then put a little bit of chocolate frosting on the tip of each one of the noses and put them on top of the cupcakes, and brought them. Those were my 'brown nose cupcakes.' And guess what? I got [the job]."

Owen believes that having a sense of humor and knowing how to have fun helped him get the job he was seeking. "Who wants to work in a place where something that simple and that human is frowned upon? I don't!"

One thing that Owen learned while working at Southwest's head-quarters is that, while everyone has a sense of humor, each person's style is different. "Everybody gets it, to some level. Not everybody has that huge, incredibly huge laugh that Herb Kelleher has, and Colleen too, for that matter. Some people's sense of fun and sense of humor is much more introverted, and that's OK."

He explains that the trade-off is that everybody at Southwest is working extremely hard, so, as long as they remain productive, exhibit-ing a sense of humor is encouraged.

Probation

At Southwest, there is a six-month probationary period before a new hire becomes a full-fledged, full-time employee. Barrett often tells her direct employees that they are always on probation. "That's kind of something she always leaves out there hanging so that you'll always realize that, no matter how long you've been here, that doesn't mean that you're better than anyone else," Shubert explains. "You're always required to perform and have the right kind of attitude at all times."

During his probationary period at Southwest Airlines, Shubert found that he wasn't as good on the telephones as he and his bosses would have liked. He was a better writer than customer relations tele-phone representative. His bosses recognized this as well, so he was shifted from the telephone position to the writer position within the Customer Relations Department. "During that probationary period," he says, "I would have to say that I was held to the same standards as everyone else. My attitude towards the company was fantastic. In fact, they said that they wanted to keep me on because my attitude was great, it's just that my telephone skills were not as polished as they wished they could have been."

One of the problems Shubert encountered during his time as a tele-phone representative was difficulty dealing with customers who would insult Southwest Airlines. He loved the company too much, and it was difficult to hear a person put down the company that had recently hired him, and at which his wife had already worked for more than seven years. Even from the beginning of his first days at Southwest, Shubert loved the company and only wanted the best for it. "I would

Consistency

Another way Southwest focuses on its employees is by smoothing their entry into its corporate culture. Southwest's manager of online relationships and special projects, Brian Lusk, says that the consistency of Southwest's culture is one attribute of the company that appealed to him when he was working for another airline and he decided to try to get a job at Southwest Airlines. "That was the thing about Southwest: the culture has been a constant," he says. "Somebody starting with Southwest today in 2009, I think they would have pretty much the same experiences I had in 1995. In fact, we've tried to actually improve the way we bring new hires into the company."

---

have to say, using a mild term, I was rather 'defensive' at times when customers would come down on Southwest. Of course, that's not a very good tack to take as a customer relations telephone representative." Although he says he was successful as a telephone representative about 97 percent of the time, he took customers' negative comments about the company too personally to succeed in that role.

While he had trouble keeping his personal feelings about the company from coming through as defensiveness while talking to customers on the telephone, Shubert's attitude was right for the company, so he made it through his probationary period and found himself in a new role for which he was better suited. By putting him into a writing position, Southwest found it had an employee with the right skill set to succeed.

Shubert is grateful that his bosses stood by their belief in hiring him more for his attitude than his aptitude. "It's the kind of company that doesn't want to throw out the baby with the bath water," he explains. "They didn't want to discard a good attitude and a good skill set just because you were unable to succeed in a specific discipline. At least you were trying. The attitude was there."

Because neither Southwest nor Shubert was optimally benefiting from the current work arrangement, the company put him first and found another role in which he could serve the company with his positive attitude. This is yet another example of the company's focus on employees that leads to better customer care.

The On-Boarding Team

One of the ways Southwest Airlines has tried to improve the experiences of new employees is through a team of employees that is brought together to do just that. The company's people come together to create an "On-Boarding Team" that welcomes new hires aboard what the company calls "the flight of their life." Southwest started the On-Boarding Group in 2006 to connect new employees with the company, reduce first-year turnover, and enhance the company's corporate culture. This group involves new hires in online orientations and lunches with company leaders such as CEO Gary Kelly to engage employees and teach them about Southwest's unique corporate culture and how to live the "Southwest Way."

Rubber Duck Derby

To celebrate the success of Southwest's On-Boarding Team, the company held a Rubber Duck Derby on May 22, 2008. Five thousand rubber ducks were unleashed into SeaWorld San Antonio's Castaway Cruisin' at Lost Lagoon while hundreds of Southwest Airlines employees watched. The Rubber Duck Derby was presented by Southwest's On-Boarding Team to celebrate the success of the On-Boarding program. Each duck was numbered, and each number represented a Southwest Airlines employee who would sponsor a new Southwest employee that year. Ducks were purchased by current employees to raise money to give the new employees a "Southwest kit," which included a lanyard, a Southwest T-shirt, and a personalized note welcoming them to the Southwest family. After racing through a mile of obstacles and rapids, the first twenty-five ducks that crossed the finish line won prizes. To show their appreciation to SeaWorld for hosting the event, Southwest donated $1,000 to the SeaWorld/Busch Gardens Conservation Fund.

"They've Had to Walk the Walk"

To help its people move up in the company, Southwest posts all open jobs internally first before reaching out of the company to hire new people. This shows its people that it cares about their advancement in the company and in their own careers. Many of the company's senior officers have moved up to their positions from other internal jobs. Some of them even started as ticket agents, as reservations agents, or on the ramp moving baggage. Even CEO Gary Kelly moved up from his position as controller and then chief financial officer of the company. But if nobody in the company has the specific skill needed for a job opening, the company will then look outside Southwest for qualified candidates.

Southwest employee Brian Lusk says the fact that the company moves many of its people up internally makes Southwest very appealing to him: "It does a couple of things. One, it shows that your career path is really only limited by your ability and your flexibility, if you need to move or relocate. On the one hand, that's one benefit. And the other benefit is that you've got people in top leadership positions where they've had to walk the walk [and do] what you're doing now."

THE GOLDEN RULE

Brian Lusk says that he could talk for hours describing Southwest's corporate culture, but it really comes down to one thing: an "emphasis on the individual. Each employee is important." He says this includes being treated with respect and having coworkers treat each other and the company with respect. He adds, "The Golden Rule is one of our key values. For a company to use that—to treat other people the way you want to be treated—that says a lot, and then to actually do it."

Another part of Southwest's corporate culture that appeals to Lusk is its emphasis on encouraging a fun-loving attitude among employees: They work hard and they play hard. This combination of many celebrations and hard work make it a place that attracts employees and customers. He points out that many employees work late on weekdays and come into work on the weekends because they want to help each other and the company succeed.

Employees live their culture on a day-to-day basis, while at work and away from work, and the company rewards them for their dedication by helping them feel important and improve themselves, their social networks, and their careers. "If you had to narrow it down," Lusk says, "for me, . . . it's just the fact that each person does matter and each person can make a difference and each person is appreciated for that. I mean, I've had more 'Thank you's' and 'Good job's' here than I'd ever had at the other job. That doesn't mean that you aren't counseled on ways to do better or if you make mistakes, but it's a good balance."

Like Lusk, Jon Shubert is a dedicated employee who believes that Southwest has changed the world in many important ways. It has also changed both of their careers for the better.

Over the last twenty years, Shubert has flourished. Today, he is in charge of maintaining all of the company's writing guidelines. He also teaches business writing at Southwest's University for People, the company's training center that helps employees learn the skills they need to succeed at the airline.

SOUTHWEST'S UNIVERSITY FOR PEOPLE

The University for People is Southwest Airlines' employee-training program. Its facility is located on the first floor of Southwest's headquarters at Love Field in Dallas. It is made up of a dozen classrooms of varying sizes. Many electives are available for employees, but some courses are required for particular roles and positions in the company. Some classes are on leadership; others are on computer skills. Shubert teaches the class on writing skills.

Southwest's University for People fills about 22,000 square feet of a former airplane hangar. It provides training for new employees and for current employees who need new skills or refresher courses. It also offers management training for employees who are ready to move up the corporate ladder. In addition to its classrooms, it also has a mock aircraft fuselage where flight attendants can practice their jobs, honing their skills for navigating through the tight work environment onboard a Boeing 737.

New ticket takers are also trained at the University for People. A mock ticket counter in the training center allows those who deal with boarding passengers to learn how to work with queues of travelers and the occasional uptight customer.

New hires spend time at the University for People learning about the company's origins through classroom instruction and videos. In one video, they watch Southwest's founder Herb Kelleher in action, attending a party dressed up as Elvis Presley, and leading the company through its early days.

Shubert teaches a variety of writing classes at the University for People. One of them is "Business Writing," which is an elective for students who would like to learn to master the skills used by the writers on Southwest's staff. He explains, "I'm responsible for maintaining the consistency of all the written product at Southwest Airlines, especially what comes out of the executive office."

JON SHUBERT'S CAREER PROGRESSION

"Coloring outside the Lines"

To reach his current level, after leaving his job as a telephone representative, Jon Shubert started writing letters for customers in Southwest's Rapid Rewards frequent flyer program. He held this position for about a year, experimenting with new approaches to customer communications, when Colleen Barrett noticed his innovative approach. He explains, "Colleen noticed that I was kind of 'coloring outside the lines,' which is what we call it here, so she gave me several types of letters that were a little more difficult." His success with these types of assignments, such as company responses to certain unusual frequent flyer issues, led to even more challenging jobs.

The idea of "coloring outside the lines" has a long history with Southwest Airlines. In the past, the company used the concept in its recruitment ads. One newspaper advertisement from Southwest's early years shows a boy being disciplined by his teacher for coloring outside the edges of a coloring-book picture of a dinosaur. The advertisement's tagline says, "Brian shows an early aptitude for working at Southwest Airlines. . . . At Southwest Airlines, you get check pluses for breaking the mold—for 'coloring outside the lines.' "

This type of outside-the-box thinking helped Shubert move up in his role as a writer at Southwest. Barrett recognized his ability to use his creativity and love for the company to communicate with customers through his strong writing skills, so she moved him into Southwest's executive offices. There he joined the team of writers in the company's Executive Office Customer Communications Department. In this role, he wrote letters on behalf of Barrett and then-President, Chairman of the Board, and CEO Herb Kelleher. Shubert says that while he was working with the company's top people, he became very comfortable in that position, which he held for nearly three years. After a series of promotions, he became manager of that department in 1994, working with six writers and the director of the department.

Managing Others

From that management position, Shubert moved into another management position. This time he was made a manager of project development and training. In this role, he was in charge of creating proofing standards for all of the writing done at Southwest Airlines.

As a company that likes to help its people develop by giving them more and more challenges to see what they can do to learn and grow, Shubert was then made a manager in the Executive Office Administrative Services Department. Here he moved out of the Writing Department and into a job where he was more of an administrative organizer of the executive office, including all of its different departments. Although he was taking on these new challenges, he was still receiving writing assignments from Barrett, who knew that he was very good at certain types of writing. Shubert says that even today he receives the occasional request from Barrett to write something for her, which he likes because it helps him keep his chops up.

A few years later, Shubert was promoted from that manager position into his current job as director of executive office administrative services. He now spends much of his days proofreading the variety of documents that continually work their way through Southwest's system, teaching at Southwest's University for People, and performing many of the same types of jobs he did as a manager in the administrative services department. Today, he is also in charge of the budgets of not only the executive office but also the Communications Department. Another job he holds is maintaining the company's corporate records. Southwest's Distribution Services Department, including the print shop, mailroom, and shipping and receiving dock, also reports to Shubert.

Individuality

Wearing so many hats, Shubert encounters a vast variety of people and roles every single day, and this is what he loves so much about Southwest Airlines and his job there: They suit his personality. "I'm kind of different," says Shubert. "I'm kind of quirky. I have my idiosyncrasies and, you know what? Ninety-nine point ninety-nine percent of them fit perfectly at Southwest Airlines. . . . I try not to take myself too seriously, although sometimes I do, and I'm reminded immediately that I'm taking myself a little too seriously, but I think I have a very healthy sense of humor. I like to use humor in my teaching. I try to use humor as much as I can with my staff.

"And I don't hide my idiosyncrasies and my quirkiness, although from the outside it might not look professional or polished, but what the heck? That's how we are here at Southwest Airlines. We like our employees to be individuals. We like for them to bring not only their skills but also their individual personalities, as long as it's not detrimental or destructive. As long as it's constructive and helps to maintain positive relationships with our employees and our customers and all, then you're well accepted."

Shubert adds that he's always felt well accepted at Southwest, which is why he's been there for more than two decades. Long before he joined the company as an employee, he says that he knew that his personality would be accepted and welcomed by the people within the company because he had experienced the company through his wife and the people with whom she worked.

Changing the World

This welcoming attitude toward people's individual differences is one of Shubert's "top ten" reasons why Southwest Airlines is a corporation that has changed the business world. He says the airline is famous for "allowing employees to be themselves, to be individuals, to bring their personalities, their skill sets, their idiosyncrasies, if you will, to bring all of that to bear for the better of the company, and for maintaining positive relationships with their peers and their leaders and those that report to them."

A second reason is its "brilliant leadership." This includes the smart financial decisions that the company's leaders have made that kept the company afloat in a very difficult industry while many competitors have gone belly-up.

Another aspect of Southwest that sets it apart from other companies and that makes it a role model for other companies, big and small, is its ability to develop a clear vision for the future and follow that vision. This vision of a better future helps all of Southwest's leaders and employees see a straightforward path to a successful future.

One additional way Shubert sees Southwest as a leader is through its innovations in the airline industry. For example, by rethinking the usual airline business model and reducing frills such as in-flight meals and films, as well as simplifying complex seating arrangements, the company has lowered fares, allowing air travel to move from a realm once populated primarily by wealthy businessmen to the rest of the people on the planet who could once afford to travel only by car, bus, or train. Today, many of Southwest's fares to certain destinations are below the price of a train ticket to those same places.

Spreading the Word

As one of Southwest's people who travel around the country to talk to other businesspeople about the company's unique and innovative business model, Shubert says that he could talk for hours about all of the reasons why Southwest stands out as a great role model for other organizations in all industries.

During his classes at Southwest's University for People and his discussions with other business leaders, Shubert talks about Southwest Airlines' innovative work in the airline industry, its award-winning customer-relations practices, and its employee-relations breakthroughs. "When I go and speak to other organizations or businesses, there are several topics that I like to talk about that make Southwest different from other companies, and two of them really get almost audible gasps from the audience. And it's because it's so revolutionary; it's so different from other companies.

"The first one is that, at Southwest Airlines, the employee comes first. You say that, and everyone out there that's in business goes, 'Oh my goodness! How's that possible? The customer comes first.' Well, no, not at Southwest Airlines, and it's because our mantra is, if you take care of the employee, the employee will take care of the customer, and then the customer will take care of the shareholder, and then the shareholder will take care of the company and the employees. It's a cycle."

The other topic that gets an audible gasp from the groups of people that Shubert speaks to is that "the customer is not always right." He says that this doesn't mean that Southwest mistreats its customers or refuses to listen to them. Nothing could be further from the truth. Shubert explains that, every day, Southwest answers every telephone call, letter, fax, and e-mail from its customers. "We listen to everything our customers have to say, and our customers have always felt very comfortable with telling us exactly what they think, but that does not necessarily mean that we can allow the customer to dictate to us how we should run our business."

If a customer becomes abusive, tries to cheat the system, destroys Southwest's property, interrupts Southwest's operations, abuses Southwest's people, or makes life miserable for any of his or her fellow customers, then Southwest will stand behind its people to do what they think is right. Although it rarely happens, sometimes Southwest will "fire" a customer.

"Very, very, very rarely—like maybe in the last twenty years, twice—have I seen us have to say to a customer something along the lines of, 'I'm sorry, but it doesn't look like we're going to be able to provide you with what it is that you want,'" Shubert explains. "Herb Kelleher himself, at one time, told a customer, 'I'm sorry, but this drugstore doesn't sell pianos.' In other words, if you're looking for a piano, don't be upset with us if you don't find one here because we run a drugstore. In other words, we are a transportation business, and we can't be everything to everybody, and if you're expecting us to be, then you're going to be disappointed."

Shubert adds that telling a customer that he or she is not right happens very rarely at Southwest, but if it happens, that person is still treated with dignity, even if that person needs to be told that they cannot get the type of transportation or service they are requesting.

With the support of their upper management, Southwest's people feel a sense of security that many other employees at other organizations might not feel when confronting angry or abusive customers. Thanks to a mandate that started with Kelleher's vision of a company that puts its employees first, they enjoy more autonomy and dignity in their jobs than those at companies where customers are put before their employees.

BUSINESS WRITING: SOUTHWEST STYLE

At Southwest's University for People, the company's training center where employees learn that their company puts them first so they will be empowered to serve their customers even better than they might if they were painted as second-class citizens, Jon Shubert's title is "visiting professor." Trainers and teachers on the University for People staff are called facilitators, and part-time coaches and trainers like Shubert, who work elsewhere in the company but teach occasional classes in their specialty, are called visiting professors.

Shubert's specialty is business writing in the Southwest style. After twenty years of writing for the company, reading the writing of others, and training others to write in the distinctive writing style that appears in all of Southwest's communications, Shubert has built up an expertise that is also a teachable skill, which Southwest likes to pass along to all of its writers and business communicators. Like the company itself, the Southwest style includes many quirky things that make it unique. It also gives Southwest's people extra attention.

The class is more than an elective for students at Southwest's University for People: Many leaders in the company also receive the same training in the writing seminars that Shubert conducts. A variation of Shubert's "Business Writing: Southwest Style" class is a module that he facilitates for employees in Southwest's leadership programs. One of those programs is "Leadership Southwest Style"; the other is "Managers in Training," or Southwest's "MIT Program." Shubert leads the business writing module for both of those leadership programs.

When a department leader feels that his or her people need a refresher course in the Southwest business writing style or when a group of new hires is ready for the information, Shubert helps these people discover the unusual style tips that make Southwest's communications more interesting and effective. For example, he recently worked with sixty of the company's marketing employees to help them learn the company's writing style. Today, he is in the process of training all of Southwest's Purchasing Department employees in the style.

Specific Language

While Shubert teaches his students business writing skills, they also learn much about the company's culture at the same time and how to perpetuate that culture through a specific type of written language. "Even our writing style reflects our culture," he explains. "For example, we capitalize the *E* in 'Employee,' the *C* in 'Customer,' the *S* in 'Shareholder,' because those three people groups represent the most important people groups at Southwest Airlines: Employees, Customers, and Shareholders." He says they want those terms to "jump off the page at you." He adds, "We respect these people groups. We appreciate them. They contribute to our bottom line here at Southwest. It's part of our culture to recognize them in a special way in our writing."

Another way that Southwest's writing style reflects the company's corporate culture is by capitalizing all company positions when they are referenced in any corporate communications. For example, a Southwest pilot is always a *Pilot*, but when a pilot from another airline is written about, that pilot is only referred to with a lowercase *p*. This same rule applies to Southwest Employees, Flight Attendants, Reservations Agents, and Ramp Agents, separating them from the employees, flight attendants, reservations agents, and ramp agents of other airlines. "That's part of our culture, too," explains Jon Shubert, "and we're able to present that to the world."

Language Southwest Style

The Southwest business writing style includes formulating terms in a unique way. For example, other airlines hyphenate the word "check-in," but Southwest's writers spell the word "checkin" with no hyphen. "Why is that?" Shubert asks. "Well, one of the reasons is because we're kind of different. We do a lot of things differently than other airlines and other companies, and you know what? That's worked for us for thirty-eight years. But another reason we do that is because it sets us apart from other companies." All of the training material and press releases that are issued by Southwest include this unique style of writing. When Southwest refers to itself in these documents, it is not just a company, it is "the Company" and "the Low-Fare Leader." Capitalizing the words it uses in its communications differently and developing its own terminology to describe its operations are just two more ways that Southwest Airlines perpetuates its unique culture. This unusual language style also provides Shubert and other leaders at Southwest with many opportunities to spread that culture. He explains, "As a leader, I have a captive audience. You better believe I'm going to talk as much about Southwest Airlines' culture as I can." This unique language is just another connection that holds Southwest's corporate culture together.

SPREADING THE CULTURE

As a leader at Southwest, Shubert takes every opportunity he can to spread the culture of the airline to the students in his classes at the University for People. These include people—both new to the company and long-time employees—from different levels and a variety of departments. "They're going to get a taste of their culture because they're going to watch me up there sometimes making an idiot of myself to drive home a point, but that's part of my personality, and that's part of my fun-loving attitude. That's part of my sense of humor. I say some pretty off-the-wall things. The thing is, though, even though they're off-the-wall, hopefully they're funny, but at least it will get them to listen and to remember."

Shubert says this is the same type of attitude that pervades the aircraft when Southwest's flight attendants give their emergency briefings to passengers before their flights. When humor is used effectively in a presentation, it can hold people's attention better than almost any other communication device.

Southwest Airlines and its people, by embracing a culture that encourages humor and a fun-loving attitude at work, have mastered the art of getting people's attention and holding it during learning situations, both on the plane and off. Jokes and a relaxed atmosphere keep Southwest's employees happy and productive because they feel like they can express themselves at work. This keeps customers coming back because they like this type of environment when they are flying, an activity that can often become stressful for a variety of reasons. The levity created by Southwest's staff helps to offset some of that tension in a healthy way that helps them share some common humanity while getting from one place to another.

"Part of our culture is using humor whenever you can to perpetuate it," explains Shubert.

PASS BUREAU

Training at Southwest Airlines does not stop at the doors of the University for People, nor is it limited to only Southwest's employees. Sometimes the company's training extends to the families of the people who work for Southwest.

For example, Southwest Airlines helps its employees use their free-flight privileges through its Pass Bureau, which acts as an internal travel agent for Southwest employees, helping them fly on Southwest as well as on other airlines that offer discounts to Southwest's employees and family members.

While helping employees schedule their many standby flights and their vacation travel plans, the Pass Bureau also helps the other people who use the employee flight benefits get the most from the company's perks. To do this, Southwest's Pass Bureau recently held a Parents Day at its headquarters in Dallas for the parents of employees. Since parents are allowed to fly Southwest flights just like their children who work at Southwest, Southwest decided to help parents figure out the travel privileges that they get thanks to their sons and daughters.

Airline employees and their immediate families can fly standby. This means they fly without paying. In the industry, this is also called flying on a "nonrevenue" or "non-rev" basis. Some employees join an airline so they can fly whenever they get the chance. Whenever a seat is available that a customer does not need, a Southwest employee or one of his or her immediate family members can ride in that seat for free.

Southwest doesn't refer to these free flights as a "benefit." Instead, they call them a "privilege" to emphasize the fact that it can be taken away if it is misused. Each employee is given strict guidelines that must be followed when flying for free. Number one on the list of guidelines is a reminder that customers are the lifeblood of the company, so serving those customers must remain paramount.

PRODUCTIVITY THROUGH FUN

Just as Southwest helps the parents of employees use their time more productively when they fly standby, it also helps its employees work more productively on the job by putting policies in place that allow them to be themselves at work.

Parents Day

Every year, parents of Southwest Airlines employees are invited out to the company's headquarters to learn more about their free flights, a benefit that is extended to employees' parents and other immediate family members. Pass Bureau manager Robert Douceau says that the annual Parents Day is an opportunity for Southwest to share information and some of its culture with people who are not employees but still enjoy free flight privileges. Along with no-cost flights at Southwest, those privileges also include being eligible for discounts on other carriers' flights. To learn how to become better travelers on Southwest, parents are walked through the many processes that they might encounter, "from listening to security documents, to getting on the plane, and being patient," adds Douceau.

Every year, more and more people show up to Parents Day. In 2008, more than three hundred parents of employees showed up at Parents Day to learn more about Southwest's travel privileges and, as Douceau says, "the right way to fly standby."

At Southwest, productivity and a fun-loving attitude go hand in hand. Thanks to its use of humor and the fun-loving attitudes of its employees, Southwest Airlines has a long history and reputation as one of the most productive airlines in the industry. Working with fewer employees per aircraft than almost all of its competitors, Southwest keeps its prices low by keeping its employee costs low, which includes keeping its employees working very productively. Southwest's leadership has found that a positive corporate culture and a fun-loving work environment help to increase the productivity of its employees.

As Jon Shubert explains, "Our financial history bears out that whatever we've been doing over the last thirty-eight years has worked, and what we've been doing is working hard and playing hard." When he talks about having fun, Shubert makes it clear that he is not talking about horseplay or childishness but rather about levity and good-natured interactions: "Herb Kelleher has always said that 'having fun frees your mind and allows you to be innovative. It allows you to be even more productive. It allows you to think more clearly.'"

Having Fun at Work

Although Southwest dispenses with rigid rules that stifle an employee's ability to act as an individual, Shubert points out that safety is still a number-one priority at Southwest. "If you can innovate—if you can do something differently and it's more efficient than the way we've always done it—then more power to you," he says. For example, if ramp agents on the tarmac hauling luggage back and forth can find a way to have fun with their physically demanding job by making it a game to keep it accurate and to keep people alert, then Southwest's leadership welcomes their innovations to the system.

As a leader of the company's mailroom and print shop, Shubert sees Southwest benefiting from this fun approach to work, and he believes Southwest's employees benefit from the freer work atmosphere. How does the company create this type of environment where people are happier and more productive in their jobs than those at other airlines? Shubert says it starts at the beginning.

Hiring for Attitude

When he speaks to other company leaders about Southwest's corporate culture, Shubert says he hears astonished gasps from his audience when he makes the statement: "We only hire the kinds of people that we can detect already have a fun-loving attitude, a productive attitude, and want to be the best they can at work, and also like to have fun."

Southwest's leaders ask prospective employees interview questions that are designed to help find the fun-loving yet productive people they seek to build the company's unique workforce. Questions that help them discover this trait in employee prospects include "How have you used humor to overcome an awkward or uncomfortable situation at work?" and "How have you used humor in your workplace to try to become more efficient or a more productive team?"

In Southwest's print shop, Shubert explains, Southwest's employees understand that when they are working hard, they are contributing not only to Southwest's bottom line but also to their own futures and job security. He says Southwest's leadership helps employees feel this way: "We are always appreciating our employees. We're always telling them they can have fun, as long as it's constructive and leads to productivity. But we start out by hiring those kinds of people to begin with."

Of course, Southwest demands the highest aptitudes of its pilots, airplane maintenance workers, and flight attendants. But for other types of positions, Shubert echoes Kelleher's belief that Southwest can always train its employees for aptitude, so it hires for attitude and then trains its people for other skills later on. "You start out with fun-loving people who want to be productive but who also want to have fun: Work hard, play hard. We start out with those people," Shubert says.

FAMILY

While Shubert has been married to a Southwest employee since starting at the company more than twenty years ago, he says that he feels like many of his fellow employees at Southwest have become part of his family over his time with the company. This feeling develops because people are always there for each other when they need support, whether they are in the workplace, sitting behind their desks, or in their personal lives. If an employee has a crisis or celebration in his or her family or personal life, Southwest's employees make themselves available to help however they can.

Shubert explains, "If there's something going on in their life, if they allow you to know about that, then you either celebrate with them, or you grieve with them, or you're happy with them, or you're sad with them. That's what family does." He adds that the sense of family at Southwest goes even further. "We have a pretty healthy sense of understanding and forgiveness of your shortcomings." As long as these shortcomings are not detrimental or destructive, he notes, forgiveness is all part of the family spirit at the company.

All of the many activities of the Internal Customer Care Department demonstrate just how far Southwest is willing to invest in keeping that family spirit alive within its corporate culture. Maintaining contact with and supporting employees who have life events is one way Southwest shows that it cares about its people. Births, marriages, terminal illnesses, graduations, and other big moments in people's lives are when family members stick together. Southwest acknowledges this human connection that people need and formalizes it by creating roles within its system to show people how important they are to the company.

"The sense of family is that, whatever happens to you also happens to us, and we want to make sure you know that we're there for you in thick and thin, good or bad, healthy, wealthy, or not," Shubert observes. As the father of a twenty-four-year-old daughter and a twenty-two-year-old son, a senior and a junior at Texas A&M, respectively, Shubert has seen firsthand how much Southwest extends its caring to its employees and their family members: "When [my children] both graduated from high school, they got very nice acknowledgments and a nice little gift from Colleen [Barrett] and Herb [Kelleher], our president and chairman of the board at the time. When they have succeeded at something in college or when they have gone through something that my wife and I have made known, then that is acknowledged by either a card or some kind of acknowledgment."

Last year, when he was fifty-three years old, Shubert was in the hospital for the first time in his adult life with a touch of diverticulitis, a common digestive tract disorder. During his stay in the hospital, he recalls that he received "a very nice card and a very nice little blanket" as recognition of the company's concern about his condition. He says that he knows that Southwest would be behind him if anything were to ever happen to him or a member of his family, which gives him

"Spousewest" Airlines

As a married couple with both spouses working at Southwest Airlines, Jon Shubert and his wife are not alone. As of 2009, Southwest actually had 1,328 married couples that work within the company. Put another way, 2,656 Southwest employees have spouses who also work for the company.

peace of mind. The airline does this, he believes, not only because it is the right thing to do but also because the people in the company truly care. "They have the employee in mind constantly, and they care about what goes on in every employee's life, because of that sense of family."

Since Southwest's Internal Customer Care Department began seven years ago, Shubert has experienced the work of the people in that department firsthand. He says that he deeply appreciates the fact that Southwest employs people who have the job of making sure that every member of the Southwest family, as well as each member of the employees' extended families, feels like someone cares about them. "That makes us a lot less of a corporation and a lot more of a family," Shubert declares.

Chapter Nine

Customer Service, Blogging, and Security at Southwest

CUSTOMER SERVICE

Some companies settle for "customer service with a smile." Southwest Airlines, on the other hand, goes the extra mile by transforming traditional customer service policies with a more powerful twist that has helped it leave its competitors far behind. Instead of dictating how its employees must serve the company's customers, Southwest allows its employees to entertain and serve its customers using whatever talents and skills they can muster, as long as they make them happy.

For example, flight attendants don't simply serve customers by demonstrating seatbelts and serving food and drinks on Southwest's flights. Some of them improve their flights dramatically by singing or telling jokes. One celebrated flight attendant named David Holmes even raps to the travelers on his flights. His talents can be seen in a video called "Flight Attendant Doing Raps!!" which has been posted on YouTube since March 14, 2009.[1]

The Rapping Flight Attendant

At the beginning of the YouTube video, Holmes welcomes passengers aboard Southwest Airlines Flight 372 to Oklahoma City: "Those of you who have flown Southwest before know that we do things a little differently here at Southwest. Some of us tell jokes, some of us sing, some of us just stand there and look beautiful. I unfortunately can do none of those. So here's the one thing that I do know how to do. We're going to shake things up a little bit. I need a little audience participation. Otherwise, this is not going to go over well at all. So, here's what I need, especially you guys in the front because you know what's coming. Alright. I need a beat!"

As the video shows the curious faces of passengers who seem to be interested but a little baffled by the impending performance, the flight attendant proceeds: "All I need you to do is stomp and clap and

I'm going to do the rest, because I've had five flights today, and I just cannot do the regular boring announcement again, otherwise I'm going to put myself to sleep. So, you guys with me? Alright. So, give me a stomp, clap, stomp, clap. Come on: stomp, clap, stomp, clap. Stay on beat there. There you go. Keep that going."

By this time, the majority of the passengers on the flight are clapping their hands and stomping their feet together and laughing to each other, while others are still placing their carry-on bags in overhead bins and finding their seats. Then the flight attendant starts his rap:

> This is Flight 372 on SWA.
> The flight attendants on board serving you today:
> Theresa in the middle. David in the back.
> My name is David, and I'm here to tell you that,
> shortly after takeoff, first things first,
> there's soft drinks and coffee to quench your thirst.
> But if you want another kind of drink, then just holler.
> Alcoholic beverages will be four dollars.
> If a Monster Energy Drink is your plan,
> that will be three dollars and you get the whole can.
> We won't take your cash. You've got to pay with plastic.
> If you have a coupon, then that's fantastic.
> We know you're ready to get to new places.
> Open up the bins, put away your suitcases.
> Carry-on items go under the seat
> in front of you so none of you have things by your feet.
> If you have a seat on a row with an exit
> we're going to talk to you, so you might as well expect it.
> You've got to help evacuate in case we need you.
> If you don't want to, then we're gonna reseat you.
> Before we leave, our advice is:
> Put away your electronic devices.
> Fasten your seatbelt, then put your trays up.
> Press the button to make the seat back raise up.
> Sit back, relax, have a good time.
> It's almost time to go so I'm done with the rhyme.
> Thank you for the fact that I wasn't ignored.
> This is Southwest Airlines. Welcome aboard![2]

A round of enthusiastic applause, hearty laughter, and appreciative smiles follows his rap. Passengers acknowledge that this is a different airline indeed! Holmes adds, "Thank you very much for my beat. I appreciate that. You will not get that on United Airlines, I guarantee you."

So far, the video, posted on YouTube by the twenty-four-year-old "CTW520" from Toronto, Canada, has been viewed more than two million times! After the video began to circulate and receive national attention, Holmes was invited to perform his rap on Jay Leno's *Tonight Show*.

David Holmes

On Gadling.com's "Galley Gossip" blog, Heather Poole interviewed David Holmes on May 8, 2009. After being introduced as Southwest Airlines' rapping flight attendant, Holmes explains that he calls both the San Francisco Bay Area and Chicago his hometowns. When asked about the support he receives from his fellow employees at Southwest for his rapping on flights, he states that he is not surprised about the positive reaction he gets from them. "I felt very comfortable that this was a good reflection of the culture that [Southwest Airlines] promotes," he says. Holmes, who was a ramp agent for three years before becoming a flight attendant and now flies about 150 trips each month, says that his advice for other flight attendants is simple: "A small amount of effort can really brighten someone's day."[3]

Holmes' attitude falls perfectly in line with Southwest Airlines' corporate culture, which encourages employees to use their personal talents and skills to serve the company's customers. Southwest recognizes that songs, jokes, or raps not only allow employees to express themselves at work but also make customers happy, which benefits the company, employees, and their customers.

Community Service

On June 28, 2009, Southwest celebrated its first flights from New York City's LaGuardia Airport. The theme of the day's festivities was "New Service, New Attitude, New York." David Holmes was invited to serenade the company's customers and employees while they dined on New York–style bagels.

At a news conference about the event, Senior Vice President of Operations Greg Wells spoke to customers, employees, and the media. At LaGuardia, Wells said, "Southwest Airlines is celebrating a truly momentous occasion today. Finally New York travelers can experience our unmatched record in customer service and our phenomenally low fares at an airport close to where they work and play."

Beyond its celebration at LaGuardia, however, Southwest's employees also ventured out into the New York City community to demonstrate the spirit that sets the airline apart from all others. One of the activities that employees organized to commemorate the airline's new LaGuardia service and to introduce the Southwest brand to New Yorkers was to clean up the grounds of Flushing Meadows Corona Park, the largest park in the New York City borough of Queens.

As Wells explained, "Southwest Airlines is dedicated to getting involved in the communities we serve. Today we're cleaning up Flushing Meadows Park, and our employees will be mentoring at MS-8 New Prep Middle School here in Queens in the coming school year—just one more way Southwest can bring its vivacious spirit to New York City."

With the addition of New York City to its roster, Southwest Airlines, the nation's largest carrier in terms of domestic passengers enplaned, increased its service to sixty-six cities in thirty-three states. By the end of 2009, it was also to begin service to Boston's Logan Airport and to Milwaukee. With the addition of these new cities, the company's thirty-five thousand employees would be operating more than 3,300 flights every day.

Listening

To serve them better, in the air and in their communities, Southwest Airlines listens to its customers. To make this happen on a daily basis, the company employs people whose job it is to stay in touch with the public through letters, e-mails, phone calls, and online.

One person who keeps in touch with the opinions and ideas of Southwest's customers online is Brian Lusk, Southwest's manager of online relationships and special projects. With his eyes and ears on the Internet, Lusk works hard to keep the company abreast of any information that it can use to serve its customers better.

Lusk has a wide variety of tasks that he performs regularly, but the main portion of his time goes toward working on Southwest's Web log, *Nuts About Southwest* (blog.southwest.com). Readers of the blog will recognize his name as a main contributor to its content, but Lusk is also extremely active behind the scenes as well, managing content on the site, moderating contributions to the site, and mining the Internet for useful company feedback.

Valuable Feedback

Some of the sites that Lusk visits regularly for valuable feedback include those with large Southwest followings, such as FlyerTalk.com, a site for frequent flyers of various airlines. Each airline, including Southwest, has its own forum on the site. When customers make comments or suggestions about Southwest's products, Lusk helps the company stay on top of their opinions and ideas, acting on them when appropriate.

Another place on the Internet where Lusk gets ideas and takes suggestions is Airliners.net, where "aviation geeks" get together and discuss the current state of the airline business in informative open forums.

With his in-depth knowledge of the airline business, learned over many years as a communications specialist at Southwest, Lusk proofreads and edits many of Southwest's internal publications. He also helps to coordinate the book projects in which the company gets involved.

Take Customer Suggestions Seriously

Southwest knows how to turn customer input into policies and procedures the company can use to improve its services and enhance its business strategy. For example, for its entire history, Southwest has always had open seating, which means that customers line up at the gate, board the plane, and take any seat that they want: first come, first served. But some customers disliked the difficulty that this sometimes created, such as the problem of leaving the line to use the restroom or get food. If you lost your place in line, you would have to move to the back of the line and accept fewer choices of seats.

Listening to customer requests, complaints, and suggestions, Southwest decided to experiment with a new way to board its planes a few years ago. Lusk explains: "We started testing assigned seating, because up to that point, it was the most requested amenity that we didn't offer from customers. We'd get a lot of letters and comments asking us why we don't have assigned seating, so we went ahead."

To test out the customer idea of assigned seating at Southwest, a procedure that it had never tried before, the company started to experiment with assigning seats on its airplanes flying out of San Diego. CEO Gary Kelly posted a message on the Southwest blog describing the testing that was going on in San Diego.

The reaction was surprising. "We were kind of taken aback," Lusk recalls, "because all of a sudden we started hearing from our long-time customers begging us not to change it, that they liked being able to select their own seat on the airplane." Many previously silent customers spoke up to express their opinions on the matter. Lusk says that some of these pleas from customers were extremely emotional. "These were people who just took [open seating] for granted, so we never heard from them, but when they found out that we were looking at changing it, they spoke up."

Seating Arrangements

Another thing that leaders at Southwest learned, once the company had opened up the dialogue on the subject of internal changes with its customers, was that they had other ideas about the company's seating arrangements. "Another thing that came out of that was, along with their plea to save it, that they were asking us to modify the way we boarded the airplane. They were getting tired of having to stand in line for a long time just to ensure a good seat. Out of that we came up with a couple of improvements in our boarding process where we now assign people boarding groups of only five customers."

Open Seating

Many of Southwest's employees have vast experience in the airline industry, which helps them better understand how Southwest is changing the business. Before joining Southwest Airlines, Brian Lusk, Southwest's manager of online relationships and special projects, worked at Delta Air Lines for eighteen and a half years, starting in 1976. This broad experience in the industry gives Lusk a seasoned perspective on the history and customers of Southwest Airlines. For example, he knows that open seating, whether in groups or first-come, first-served, makes sense for Southwest's business strategy.

When he started at Delta Air Lines, customers for long flights could pick their seats by walking up to a board that held tabs for each seat on the airplane. Each passenger physically pulled off a tab for his or her seat to reserve it. On shorter flights, service agents would simply pull off a tab for each customer to assign him or her a seat. After that, when new technology entered the picture, service agents used computers to assign passenger seats. Most airlines followed that path. On less-booked flights, many of them would allow passengers to choose their own seats after boarding. But Southwest made it a policy on all flights.

By boarding people five at a time, nobody has to stand in line for too long before the gate opens, and nobody has to rush to the gate once it does. Instead, customers can relax, have a cup of coffee, and casually wait until their group is called to the gate to board the plane.

The idea for new seating arrangements for customers that Southwest implemented in 2007 was something no other airline had ever tried before. While a few airlines have experimented with open seating, most airlines still have assigned seating.

Respond to Requests

Southwest also listened to its customers and acted on their suggestions when it changed the way it publishes and announces its new flight schedules.

On January 24, 2007, Bill Owen, the head planner in Southwest's Scheduling Department, posted a blog entry that explained the economic and customer service reasons that the company posts its schedules only four or five months before its flights. Since many customers like to plan their vacations many months in advance, some of them wrote in to Southwest Airlines to tell the company that it would like more lead time in its schedules so they could plan their flights further ahead of time. Many other airlines publish their schedules about eleven months ahead of time, so customers were curious as to why Southwest does not do the same thing.

Owen's note really stirred up some strong opinions from the airline's customers. Some pointed out that Southwest's schedules often came out as little as three months in advance, which made it even harder to plan their business and vacation trips ahead of time. They also protested that Southwest did not tell its customers when its new schedules would be released, which made it even harder to anticipate where and when its planes would fly. They did not like to have to guess when flights would take place. The blog received nearly six hundred comments on the topic. This alerted Southwest to a problem that it needed to address.

Less than three months later, Southwest Airlines responded to the problem. The Planning Department made a pledge to try to have at least four months, or 120 days, of schedules available to customers at all times. The department's leaders also told customers and employees that they would "push the maximum available inventory from 180 days to between 190 and 200 days of inventory," paying close attention to make "peak travel periods available for booking as far in advance as possible."

Customers and employees overwhelmingly said they liked the company's response. Lusk adds, "As a result of that, our schedule planning leadership now publishes the schedule opening dates on Southwest.com."

"You Flamed. We Changed."

To describe the new, revised policy to Southwest's customers and the readers of his blog posts, Owen wrote a follow-up entry titled "I Blogged. You Flamed. We Changed." In that post, Owen explained:

> We heard you, loud and clearly, and we reacted. I realize some of you wish we would extend the booking window even further out, and while we won't do that this "go-round" we will continue to study the issue and may, at a later time, choose to do so. In any event, I hope these changes make planning your travel on Southwest easier. Like all airlines, Southwest appreciates your business—but unlike other airlines, we LUV you, and we appreciate your honesty! Thanks for all of the responses and thank you for reading "Nuts About Southwest"![4]

BLOGGING

Southwest's decision to start its own blog allows the unexplored writing and storytelling talents of many of its employees to shine,

Quick Turnarounds

Open seating makes economic sense for Southwest Airlines. As Brian Lusk explains, "We always kept open seating just because all of our studies showed it reduces your turnaround time. The quicker you can turn a flight at the gate and get it back on its way, the least money it costs you because airplanes don't make money sitting at the gate. They make money while they're flying."

Southwest Airlines, since its earliest days, has always maintained a focus on getting its aircraft to the terminal, up to the gate, unloaded, boarded with new customers, and back on its way as fast as possible. Success at doing this has created its long-lasting reputation for having the fastest turnaround times in the industry. Lusk says that turnaround times have "grown since the days of the ten-minute turns, but we can still turn around two heavily loaded flights within twenty minutes. I think twenty-five minutes is as short as we schedule right now, but we can definitely do it quicker when we have to."

With so many variables with airports, passengers, airplanes, and employees, sometimes a turnaround can last much longer than anticipated. Southwest schedules more than thirty-two hundred flights each day, and some of those can sit on the runway for longer than twenty-five minutes. But, in general, Southwest works diligently to get its airplanes landed, unloaded, reloaded, and back in the air as soon as possible. "You may need to hold it to maybe connect with another flight, or to ensure that a flight crew will be there," Lusk says, but otherwise, the company works hard to satisfy customers and maintain low fares by keeping its airplanes in the air and on schedule.

---

while also opening up the Internet to the voices and ideas of the company's customers. When Southwest started its blog in 2006, Southwest was the first airline to incorporate a full-time blog into its Web site. As of 2009, it was still one of only two airlines in the United States to do so. Southwest was also one of the first few *Fortune* 500 companies to start its own full-time blog.

Brian Lusk was one of the first bloggers at Southwest, helping the company to create an online presence when no other airline had crossed that frontier. "We were really out there pioneering away, so that was really exciting to be on the leading edge of a new way of communicating with customers," Lusk says.

From There to Here

Like many of Southwest's employees who work in its Dallas headquarters at Love Field, Lusk has been through many jobs that have brought him to his current position. He started as a reservations sales agent in Southwest's old Dallas Reservations Center. After his six-month probationary period working there, he found a job in the company's headquarters at its Ticketless Help Desk. Southwest's ticketless flying program—that is, using electronic tickets rather than paper ones—was only a year old at the time, so he helped the department work out the many bugs in its new system. "They needed a help desk for our Reservations Center so the airports could call if they had a problem with the ticketing." One of his tasks was helping customers apply unused funds to new reservations, which added some complexity to the company's new program.

As a result of the success of this system and to respond to the changing marketplace, Southwest formed a new department called the Reservations Resource Center. Today, this same department is called "S.O.S.," or Source of Support. Lusk was one of the first people in this department, helping customers in any way that he could so they could get the most from their interactions with Southwest Airlines. His experiences gave him a deep knowledge of the way reservations work at an airline, as well as the customer relations issues involved in the process.

After some time in the Reservations Resource Center, Lusk still had dreams of using his writing skills in his daily job for Southwest, so when he saw an opening in the Public Relations Department, he applied. Although he didn't get that position, Vice President of Public Relations Ginger Hardage—who would become vice president of corporate communications and assume the responsibility for the culture aspects at Southwest from President Colleen Barrett in June 2008—recommended that Lusk try to get a job in the company's executive office at its headquarters, where a writing team wrote to customers. In 1997, Lusk applied for the first opening that he saw on the team. He didn't get the writing position, but he did get an editing position on the team a month later.

For the next ten years, Lusk worked on the editing team in Southwest's Culture Services Department. In 2001, he became the manager of his group.

A Blog Is Born

At the end of 2005, Lusk received an invitation to attend a meeting about the possibility of a corporate blog. Representatives from all of Southwest's customer communications groups were asked to share their ideas on blogging. He recalls, "I went to that meeting and thought it was kind of interesting. I had never really heard about blogs."

As a result of that meeting, Lusk got more involved with the new group that was forming to discuss and design Southwest's foray into blogging. He quickly became an expert on the subject. Working with RD2, a Dallas company that designs blogs, Lusk was part of the initial team that presented its findings and proposal to Southwest's Executive Planning Committee. During the presentation, the team of bloggers showed company leaders what the blog would be. They were seeking approval so they could proceed with their project, and they got it.

Once the team's plan was approved, Lusk began posting on Southwest's new blog and helping to manage the site. He did this part-time for the next two years. During this period, Southwest began merging its media departments, which led to Lusk becoming the first full-time blogger at a major airline.

Today, Southwest's blog, *Nuts About Southwest*, is a busy place. "We've had probably over two million people visit it in the first three years," Lusk estimates. Southwest's blog goes beyond customer relations. Lusk sees it as a communications and public relations portal.

Reaching Out to Customers Online

Another way Southwest reaches out to the public, and helps customers and employees reach back and share ideas and stories, is through Twitter, the popular social messaging tool that allows people to send and receive information to their cell phones, computers, and handheld devices. So far, the company has well over half a million followers, which is a very large number of people who follow the company's latest posts. New people are connecting to it every day.

The company has posted more than three thousand updates since joining the site. Whether it is telling people about contests for its Twitter followers, connecting people to photos of a Southwest cocktail napkin collection, alerting flyers to the flights on which its new wi-fi service is available, or telling people where to go to earn extra Rapid Rewards credits, Southwest's Twitter page is an active place where the company's employees and fans connect for a multitude of reasons.

The company also connects to people using a variety of other social networking sites, such as Facebook, Flickr, LinkedIn, and YouTube.

Southwest uses its Facebook page to tell customers when it is creating or changing its services, to offer them special deals, to ask them questions, and to keep them up to date on recent developments in the company.

According to *Inside Facebook*, a Web site that tracks Facebook and the Facebook platform for Web developers and marketers, Southwest Airlines is number one on its list of airlines and cruise lines that are best leveraging their Facebook pages to help travelers get to their destinations. As writer Jessica Lee explains, "According to [Internet data collector] PageData, there are a total of 1.3 million fans in [the Airlines/Ships/Trains] category of Facebook Pages with the average fans per page being just under 2,500."[5] Southwest was the top company on the list, with 70,579 fans as of mid-2009, more than twice the next nearest airline, Virgin America, and posts on its Facebook page help it to accumulate new fans almost every day of the month. These statistics show that Southwest's position as a social-media savvy company continues to pay off as it attracts passengers through a variety of Internet fronts.

Southwest also has a video department that keeps its blog populated with new videos that draw traffic from customers and potential customers. These videos include reports on the latest Southwest events, both formal and informal, and allow customers to view employees at work and at play, to watch safety inspections, and to see inside the company's operations. Many of these videos are also available on YouTube, alongside the video of Southwest's "rapping flight attendant" David Holmes.

Listening and Learning

Through its Web presence and its blog, Southwest has been able to tap into a diversity of opinions, which helps a company to survive in a rapidly changing marketplace. Along with providing the company with a wide range of points of view, Southwest blogger Lusk says the company's blog serves many purposes, but "it's mainly to have a conversation, to be out there and form a way that you can connect with your customers." He adds, "It also allows us the ability to get our message out without being filtered by the traditional media. That's been really important to us."

When Southwest posts a video on its blog, that video appears in its entirety, bypassing the editing process that often takes place when a company sends its information to another news outlet. As a result, customers get to see what Southwest wants to show them, uncut and unfiltered. The same is true for its blog posts. Instead of being edited to fit into a newspaper or magazine's news slot, posts on Southwest's blog reach customers intact, offering substantial support for the press releases it sends to traditional media outlets.

Southwest's blog has become an important tool in the company's toolkit of techniques for reaching out to its customers. Sometimes it is even more effective than traditional press releases. "We can write a blog post that provides the background to that press release and the human interest part of what brought about the press release," says Lusk. "We can put that on the blog and not have it filtered. It's a way to get our point of view and our message out the way we want it to go out."

In the region of Texas where Southwest's headquarters is located, both the *Dallas Morning News* and the *Fort Worth Star-Telegram* have aviation blogs. "They're always quoting our blog," Lusk notes. "We use Twitter to put out story ideas because a lot of our followers are reporters, so we can pitch a story idea via Twitter."

"Pulling Thread through the Needle"

At Southwest Airlines, Linda Rutherford is vice president of communications and strategic outreach. As a strong advocate for her people within the company, she believes that leadership is "lighting the path and cheering on the talent you surround yourself with as they sprint down it."

Lusk says that Rutherford describes the goal for Southwest's blog as part of "pulling the thread through the needle." In other words, Southwest's blog is part of the many different ways that the company touches customers and employees. By complementing each other, they all become a single communications tool that "makes a bigger hole" through which Southwest can reach out to people, inside and outside the company.

SECURITY

Southwest Airlines' Aviation Security Department is responsible for communicating any changes in airport security procedures to customers and employees. The department team is in charge of all things related to regulations, security, and the U.S. Transportation Security Administration (TSA). One of its goals is to interface with the government agencies in charge of counterterrorism, including the TSA and the Department of Homeland Security as well as various other federal intelligence and law enforcement agencies. Basically, the security team at Southwest Airlines keeps bad guys off of the company's airplanes.

But security at Southwest is not limited to its Aviation Security Department: Every employee in the company that is tied to customer relations and customer service in some way has a role to play. As security regulations and security procedures sometimes quickly change, customers often get very frustrated. Southwest's employees work hard to try to answer customers' questions and resolve their problems. While doing this, the members of the security team at Southwest work hard to empathize with customers and defuse difficult situations by helping customers find the solutions that can get them where they want to go. Southwest's employees-come-first policy helps them serve the company's customers.

Southwest demonstrates how it puts its employees first by creating channels that help them help their customers. By giving them the tools that can help them succeed, and giving them the right information that can help them communicate with the people with whom they work face to face, the company empowers its employees to use their best judgment when making decisions.

Members of Southwest's Security Team help to provide frontline employees with a high-level view of what's going on behind the scenes with regulations and procedures. The team offers them a direct connection to those who can help to answer any questions they might have about the ever-changing security environment in which the airline industry operates. Aviation Security Department managers also provide frontline employees with the ability to have customers contact security team members directly so they can answer any questions they might have that the frontline employees are unable to answer themselves.

The Customer Relations Department is another group of employees that helps employees answer questions and can also answer customer questions directly. If the questions are security related, those questions will funnel back to the Security Department, which can give customers the most updated information available.

At Southwest, the key to helping employees help customers is creating the proper channels of communication that get the right information to the right people at the right time.

CHANGING TIMES, CHANGING NAMES

As times change and the economic landscape shifts with the ebb and flow of the local, national, and global marketplace, Southwest adapts by examining its processes and appropriately shifting them to suit the new needs of customers. One example of Southwest's commitment to serving customers by changing with the changing times: The company recently changed the name of its Reservations Department.

At one time, the employees in Southwest's Reservations Department were the people who took calls from customers who wanted to book a flight. Over the years, new developments in the Internet and other technologies have pushed much of the work done by these people into the online world. The booking process has primarily gone digital. Telephone calls to Southwest have slowly dropped over time, and the amount of work that those involved in taking traditional phone reservations decreased, too. The calls that did come through to the Reservations Department were also different. Instead of simply booking flights, customers who called the company were more interested in the details of Southwest's policies and regulations regarding security, baggage, Rapid Rewards credits, and so on.

To deal with the changing nature of their job and the calls they were receiving, Southwest decided to make some changes. The company realized that it had a group of people who were amazing at talking on the phone and helping to serve customers, but their skills and talents needed some adjustments to help them stay productive in the new corporate environment where many of their previous customers were slowly migrating to the Internet. As a result, Southwest Airlines sent the employees from its Reservations Department to its University for People to learn new skills in other areas that would help them adapt to the new marketplace.

The company changed the name of the department to Customer Services and Support in 2008. The name change was made to reflect what the employees in the department are doing on a day-to-day basis.

Customer Services and Support

Today, employees in Southwest's Customer Services and Support Department take calls regarding any customer relations issue. Their expertise ranges from flight credit to security to frequent flyer miles to booking flights. Until recently, Southwest did not take e-mail queries from its customers, but now, with further training of its employees in Customer Services and Support, the company gladly responds quickly to customer questions sent in through the Internet.

Airlines in the United States are required by the rules of the Department of Transportation to respond to customer questions within eight weeks. But Southwest Airlines has a corporatewide goal of responding to all inquiries within four weeks, half the federal standard.

This standard was set back when traditional mail was the primary way the company corresponded with its customers who had concerns or complaints, allowing for the time it took to receive a complaint or question, research the issue, and mail a response back to the customer.

Today, e-mail makes customer correspondence much more immediate. With nearly four thousand employees on the Customer Services and Support Department's team helping to respond to e-mail questions from customers, the company is able to get answers back to customers faster than ever. While employees in the department formerly known as Reservations have changed the nature of their work and daily activities—and the name of their department has changed to the Customer Services and Support Department—they continue to use their skills and talents for serving customers, which is what they do best.

Focusing on Strengths

Along with reflecting the changes that have taken place in the work these people do, the name change to Customer Services and Support also reflects a deeper connection between employees and customers—focusing on the strengths of employees and putting them where they can best serve customers.

This revamping of a department and the roles of the employees within it demonstrates Southwest's commitment to its people. Instead of recognizing a decrease in phone reservations and firing the employees who were doing that work, and then hiring new people with Internet skills to answer questions that come in via e-mail, Southwest retrained its reservations people and kept these seasoned airline professionals who had already proven their value to the company on the payroll. Plus, it was a perfect opportunity to expand employees' horizons by giving them opportunities to learn new skills.

In addition, by helping customers get more of what they need from a single source, Southwest helps to prevent its customers from becoming irritated or unhappy, which keeps its customers coming back for more flights.

The Influence of Culture

Southwest manager Brian Lusk points out that the way Southwest Airlines treats its customers is simply an extension of the company's corporate culture. "The culture extends to our customers. You'll hear a lot of people say that anyone can copy our business model, which is flying a single type of airplane, or point-to-point service with low fares. Anyone can copy that, but they can't copy the people. And I think our customers realize that."

Chapter Ten

Leadership at Southwest

While Herb Kelleher was the top executive at Southwest Airlines, he told his fellow leaders, "Be humble; work harder than anyone else; serve your people."[1] Hard work and humility have become a powerful combination at Southwest, helping it attract employees, customers, and accolades.

This leadership philosophy has also made Kelleher one of the most admired and influential corporate leaders of all time. By successfully putting these principles to work within his company, he made Southwest Airlines a company whose approach to business has been emulated around the world by businesses in every industry and of every size.

GINGER HARDAGE

Today, one of the top leaders at Southwest Airlines who lives Kelleher's words about humble leadership and hard work is Ginger Hardage. Nearly eighteen years after she joined the company as the director of public relations, Hardage became the senior vice president of culture and communications at Southwest Airlines in July 2008. Since then, she has been in charge of Southwest's celebrated corporate culture, which was started in the company by Kelleher and institutionalized by Colleen Barrett. Hardage points out that Southwest's company culture has been largely responsible for introducing the concept of an employee-centric corporate culture to the world.

Previously, Hardage was the leader of Southwest's communications teams. However, "When Colleen stepped into a different role, and away from her official role, and became president emeritus in July of last year, I took over the culture aspect of the company as well," Hardage says.

Every day, Hardage focuses on the company's programs that perpetuate Southwest's unique corporate culture, along with its internal and external communications programs. This includes all public relations,

Ginger Hardage is senior vice president of culture and communications for Southwest. (Courtesy Southwest Airlines.)

employee communications, and charitable giving. About 120 people within the company are part of Hardage's teams.

Public Relations

Kelleher and Barrett hired Hardage as director of public relations in 1990 because of her education in public relations, her thirteen years of experience in the field, her gregarious disposition, and her positive attitude. Prior to 1990, she had been doing public relations work for other companies since she graduated from Texas Tech University in Lubbock.

"Coming to Southwest was a dream job," she explains, "because it was known then as a great place to work, and that truly hasn't changed. I need to be with a company that has a strong consumer profile because I like to be able to directly impact customers, as opposed to being a business-to-business thing."

When Hardage joined the company, Southwest was much smaller than it is today. During her two decades with the airline, her ability to have a direct impact on customers has greatly increased as the company has grown and her role within it has expanded. "Back in 1990, it was already an extremely successful and watched-after company, so it was a dream to be part of it. I was pinching myself."

Today, one of Hardage's jobs is speaking to classes of new hires in Southwest's University for People. Remembering her own reaction to hearing the news that she had been hired by the company, she says she likes to keep that feeling alive among the company's new employees: "I always remind them, 'Never forget how excited you were when you heard, and you got that call, that official offer to join Southwest Airlines,' because I think so many people do aspire to be that. You never want to lose that enthusiasm and forget what that feeling was like when you did get that job offer."

Getting Hired

Hardage says her own interview for the job at Southwest was "hysterical." Her initial interview with the company was with its founder Kelleher and President Barrett. She recalls: "I had another job, so it was after work. It went on for hours. We laughed! I felt like I made two friends. It wasn't your typical job interview by any means. It was more like being at a cocktail party, minus the cocktails. We just had such a great visit.

"But the funny thing is, Colleen told me she wanted me to talk to some officers in the company to interview me, and I didn't hear, and I didn't hear. And, finally, one day I was back at my other job. And I get this call from this guy and he says, 'You don't know me, but I'm the vice president of governmental affairs here at Southwest, and I'm sitting here with the vice president of marketing, and we're waiting on you for your nine o'clock interview.'

"I went, 'Oh my gosh! What have I done?'

"And then he started laughing. He said, 'But then we realized we didn't tell you you were supposed to be here, and we're in trouble because we were supposed to have interviewed you by now.'

"And then I had a very quick interview with both of them that day, and then got the official signoff and offer to come to work. I felt like that dream job was just passing before my eyes at that moment."

The lighthearted, informal style of business that Hardage saw among the executives at Southwest really appealed to her. Where she grew up in rural Texas, all forms of pretense—what her mother always called "putting on airs"—were extremely frowned upon. Southwest Airlines exhibited the kinds of values that she held in her own heart. "You can really be yourself," she explains. "You *have to* be yourself, and that is really something that we all put a lot of pride in. You really are able to be yourself."

Hiring Others

Today, when Hardage is hiring new people, she follows Kelleher's guidance and always tries to "hire for attitude before aptitude." One of the ways she does this is, instead of asking prospective employees "What if this situation happens?" and "What would you do?" she prompts them with the slightly different scenario: "When this happened, give me an example of what you did." She then listens to prospects tell her what they did in a specific difficult situation from their past rather than an imaginary hypothetical situation.

Another way that Southwest finds out more about a job candidate's attitude and skills is by having that person interview with many, many different people from within the company. Some have described it as a "speed dating" situation where they meet several different types of people from within Southwest during a single interviewing event.

Fitting In

Southwest's screening process can be an intense experience for job applicants. "It is not an easy interview process," Hardage admits. "We want you to meet a lot of different people. It's almost like passing you through a sieve. You're going to have an opportunity to meet a lot of different people to see how you fit in, and for you to see how you fit in as well."

In his book *Keeping the People Who Keep You in Business*, Leigh Branham writes that organizations that live by their values and mission or purpose attract the types of people who will fit in, succeed, and stay. They will also "repel those whose values are incompatible. At Southwest Airlines, for example, any job candidate who is not drawn to the company's mission to make flying a fun and pleasant experience will probably not even survive the company's careful screening process."[2]

A "fun-LUVing" atmosphere is not for everyone. Those who find such an environment uncomfortable will often take themselves out of the running for a job at Southwest early in the hiring process. On the other hand, those who enjoy working in such an environment make much better candidates for positions within the company.

Along with conducting numerous interviews with job candidates, Southwest's leaders also talk with as many references as possible for each prospect, to get to know the job candidate as a person and a potential employee. Hardage adds that she looks at each person who interviews for the company as a potential guest in her home: "I always think, Do I want to have this person over for dinner at my house? Are they going to be somebody I can work with for a long time?"

That philosophy makes sense at Southwest Airlines, because the company has a reputation for keeping its employees for a very long time, which benefits the company in innumerable ways. For example, Hardage has been with the company for nearly twenty years. Many of the people with whom she works have been with the company much, much longer.

Like Minds

When she is interviewing potential employees, Hardage looks at the long-term, big picture. "You want it to be someone that you would want to be stranded in that rowboat with, that they know that they're going to be rowing just as hard as you are. You want people of like minds."

She also looks for people who do not take themselves too seriously, so a sense of humor is a great asset. Another asset is what President Emeritus Barrett often refers to as "a servant's heart." To find these things, Hardage listens closely to the responses job candidates give to questions about what they would do when confronted with an intense situation. People who get upset easily, who always have to control situations, or who don't exhibit much flexibility will not make the cut.

"The fact that we're in the customer service business, you have to want to serve others," Hardage explains. "If you're the type of person who has always been served, you're probably not going to be a good fit here, because we are all looking for people who will do whatever it takes to get the job done, and you never know what that might be."

CHANGING THE WORLD

When Ginger Hardage takes a broad look at the important things that Southwest Airlines has accomplished and the ways it has changed the world, she says two things stand out for her. The first is the way it has transformed the way people think about air travel. "We made it affordable for people to be able to fly," says Hardage.

"When I was growing up, my family couldn't afford to fly anywhere. Airfares were extremely expensive. The only way we could go anywhere was in our car. [Southwest Airlines] not only changed leisure travel where people at the drop of a hat can afford to go to Disney World, but also businesses. We have so many businesses that tell us that if they are expanding, if they are based out of Phoenix, for example, they would probably only expand their business to cities that Southwest serves, because they knew that they could afford to travel back and forth between their various offices and make it work. We make business travel affordable as well. So, opening up the skies and really making air travel affordable was one of the huge ways that Southwest has changed the world."

She adds that Southwest has also opened up air travel beyond the United States by serving as the inspiration for other airlines across the world that emulate its low-fare business model. These companies have adapted Southwest's strategies in other countries that have never experienced air travel based on a low-cost model. In this way, Southwest has opened up the skies to people all around the globe.

Introducing the Concept of Corporate Culture

The second positive effect that Ginger Hardage believes Southwest Airlines has had on the world is the way it has brought the idea of a corporate culture to the mainstream. She explains: "If we had had Google thirty years ago, and we could have Googled 'corporate culture.' I don't think that is something that we would have found many uses of. In terms of really putting a focus on the importance of your corporate culture, I think that is something that Southwest Airlines has done through Colleen Barrett."

In other words, Southwest Airlines has put the concept of corporate culture on the map. Hardage explains that any passenger on a Southwest flight can see firsthand how the flight attendants are empowered to interact with passengers. They are encouraged to show their own unique skills and talents. They are allowed to demonstrate their unique personalities to their customers, which turns Southwest flights into more comfortable and enjoyable experiences.

"Not everybody can sing, or not everybody can tell a joke," Hardage continues, "but they may just have really a lot of empathy. Some of our flight attendants are known for their empathy and their ability to connect with the customer, so we really ask our employees to use whatever that unique talent is they have to connect with our customers." The freedom for employees to be themselves is an essential part of Southwest's celebrated corporate culture.

Hardage describes Southwest's corporate culture as an energy that helps to pull its people together toward a common goal, as opposed to many other corporations that push each other apart by encouraging internal competition.

Executives at the company are well aware of the power that putting its employees first has on its bottom line. That's why their needs are always considered when setting strategy. According to Hardage, "Every decision that we make, our employees are front and center in making that decision."

Frontier Airlines

In Hardage's view, a perfect example of the company's employee-centric decision making is the recent attempt by Southwest to acquire Frontier Airlines. In August 2009, Southwest bid on Frontier, which had filed for Chapter 11 bankruptcy protection in April 2008, but the bid was not accepted. The Associated Press reported that "Republic Airways Holdings won the bankruptcy court auction for Frontier Airlines . . . buying the Denver-based carrier for almost $108.8 million after Southwest Airlines Co.'s rival bid was rejected."[3]

"We decided to participate in the bidding in an auction process, but weren't successful because we were not willing to drop some of our contingencies that called for agreement on labor that would greatly impact our culture and our employees," Hardage explains. "We were not willing to proceed with acquiring the company if we didn't have the people issues resolved ahead of time. We didn't want to go ahead and be successful in bidding for that company if we had to make changes in our corporate culture or our people policies in order to make it work. We wanted to work those out in advance."

By dropping its bid for Frontier, Southwest's leaders demonstrated to the company's employees that they stand by their frontline people in both word and deed.

Respect

Freedom to dress informally is one aspect of work as an executive at Southwest that is different from the way other large companies do business. Hardage points out that on days when she is in the office working at her desk, she can usually be found wearing a pair of jeans and sandals.

Beyond a lenient dress code, the differences in the executive suite at Southwest go much deeper. "There is a tremendous amount of respect that everyone shows toward each other," says Hardage, "whether you're in a meeting in the boardroom or you're visiting with employees in the employee break room or in the flight attendant lounge. The same amount of respect is shown to every individual regardless of who they are in the corporation." Anyone who has ever worked in a company where he or she felt that leaders did not give employees the proper respect at work can appreciate the differences that Southwest works to create throughout its company every day.

Southwest Airlines has a traditional corporate hierarchy, but the company's organizational chart is leveled by the ways that executives and employees on the front line interact. "You have to have a hierarchy to get certain things done," Hardage explains, "but we're not dependent on it and we're very team oriented."

"I think one of the surest ways to failure at Southwest is to try to make yourself an island and not be integrated with other departments," she continues. "You could have individual success, but it's worthless if it's not reaching team goals. Everything is focused on the success of the team or the entire company."

Both Kelleher and Barrett are credited with the integration of this kind of teamwork philosophy throughout Southwest. Today, CEO Gary Kelly and his executive team have been integral in maintaining the discipline needed to keep teamwork alive across all of the functions within the company and making sure all employees do not lose sight of this prime ingredient in Southwest's success.

FRONTLINE LEADERSHIP

In Regina Fazio Maruca's book *What Managers Say, What Employees Hear*, Jody Hoffer Gittell describes how leaders at Southwest form working relationships with their employees. Gittell quotes Southwest's former executive vice president of customers, Donna Conover, who explains, "The most influential leaders in our company—aside from Herb—are the frontline supervisors."[4]

Performance measures take a backseat to cross-functional accountability. Gittell explains that Southwest Airlines made the management decision to increase supervision while reducing its emphasis on measuring the performance of its employees. To do this, the company adopted a strategy of making its people accountable across job functions:

> Cross-functional accountability increased cooperation and learning across functional boundaries by taking the focus off of finger-pointing and reducing the fear factor, and narrow spans of control allowed supervisors to engage actively in supporting coordination through coaching and feedback.[5]

Gittell concludes that the critical role of supervisors is not just their direct interaction with employees to facilitate coordination that makes them effective. Instead, she writes, "Supervisors have their biggest impact by supporting frontline employees' efforts to coordinate *directly with each other*."[6] In other words, Southwest differs from other companies in the way that leaders are more than bosses. They are the people who help their people get together and lead themselves.

Beyond Open Doors

Leaders at Southwest have an "open door" policy that keeps employees in the loop of leadership. This means that executives' and managers' doors are always open to any employee who needs to discuss a company issue with a boss who can help him or her figure out a pressing issue.

When James L. Heskett and Leonard A. Schlesinger discuss the topic of open doors in their essay "Leaders Who Shape and Keep Performance-Oriented Culture" in the book *The Leader of the Future*, they describe Southwest as an example of a company that takes open-door policies to the next level. They explain that Herb Kelleher would not just wait for employees to come to him—he would go to them. They write that going to employees enables leaders to listen better.

Another part of leadership at Southwest includes stepping back and allowing employees to make more decisions on the front line, as long as they follow one guideline: Do whatever you feel comfortable doing for the customer. Heskett and Schlesinger write:

> This requires not only that employees have the necessary latitude to act but also that they have the information and support with which to do so intelligently and the loyalty to do so in the best interests of the company as well as its customers.[7]

The coauthors also quote Kelleher, responding to a question about how he accounts for his organization's performance, who said, "I'd like to attribute it to brilliant leadership, but I can't. It's the people of the airline and their feelings for customers and one another."[8]

Giving credit where credit is due is another way that Southwest's leaders motivate their highly productive workforce. And much credit for the company's success is often directed back to the company's founders. For example, Ginger Hardage says, "I think one of the things Herb can so be credited for is really sticking to the basics and being simple in terms of our business model. That is something that's easy to say but hard to do." This means staying focused on the company's people and staying focused on customer service.

Customer Service

Keeping it simple is at the heart of Southwest's business model, which can be summed up in very few words. As Hardage says, "We're in the customer service business."

Southwest's mission statement does not contain the words *airplane* or *transportation*. Instead, the company's mission statement reads: "Dedication to the highest quality of customer service, delivered with a sense of warmth, friendliness, individual pride, and company spirit."

GARY KELLY

When Gary Kelly became CEO of Southwest Airlines in July 2004, he had already been an officer within the company for many years. Company founder Herb Kelleher was also still chairman of the company, and Colleen Barrett was still president, so his transition into the top spot was very organic, with many people around him to help him step up. Ginger Hardage recalls, "It was a long transition, so there was nothing startling about it for the organization."

When Kelly was promoted, Jim Parker had just stepped down from the CEO position. Comparing the two leaders, Hardage says they were both executive officers who had been with the company for many years and had been "steeped in Southwest Airlines" for a long time. She notes, "Gary is more gregarious, definitely, than Jim was, but we joke

In 2004, Southwest Airlines' CEO, president, and chairman of the board Gary Kelly becomes Gene Simmons from the rock band KISS for Halloween. (Courtesy Southwest Airlines.)

that we don't know anybody on the planet who is more gregarious than Herb. Gary's definitely holding his own in that category." Kelly's gregarious nature is highly visible when he participates in many of the parties and events that take place within Southwest Airlines.

LEADERSHIP STYLE

Ginger Hardage realizes that Gary Kelly's leadership style goes beyond his gregarious nature. "He's very inclusive," she says, "and decision making is team oriented. One of the things that we did early on as an executive planning team was spend a lot of time getting to know each other and understanding each other's work styles."

When Kelly became chief executive officer, Southwest Airlines hired celebrated business consultant Patrick Lencioni and his firm the Table Group to help the company's management team speed along the process of coalescing as a team. Their work helped the company and its executives make the transition to their new CEO's style as a leader.

"We spent time on Myers-Briggs, understanding those differences," Hardage explains. According to the organizational performance development firm CPP, the publisher of the Myers-Briggs Type Indicator (MBTI) assessment, the Myers-Briggs assessment is a personality inventory designed to give people information about their psychological preferences. Originally developed in the early 1940s by Isabel Briggs Myers and Katherine Cook Briggs, the Myers-Briggs assessment was developed to make Carl Jung's theory of human personality understandable and useful in everyday life. Today the MBTI tool has become the most widely-used personality assessment in the world.[9]

The MBTI tool doesn't label people as good or bad. Instead, it indicates an individual's preferences for extraversion or introversion, sensing or intuition, thinking or feeling, and judging or perceiving. After a person is tested using the MBTI, information is provided that describes the communication patterns that are effective for the people of his or her personality type.

Southwest Airlines uses the MBTI assessment tool in many ways. It is used to build teams, resolve conflict, and help develop its leadership programs by facilitating better communication among team members. The company also uses the Myers-Briggs to help employees deal with conflicts.

In addition, the Myers-Briggs tool is used at Southwest to help teams that are already working together improve their work. According to Elizabeth Bryant, director of Southwest's University for People, this tool is in ongoing use at the company: "The MBTI assessment helps leaders and teams by providing them with communication tools, helping them to recognize and celebrate their differences."[10] The results and information a team receives as a result of using the MBTI tool is then applied in the workplace to help the company get better results from its people.

Honoring the Individual

Leadership at Southwest spends much of its time honoring and understanding the individual. The MBTI helps the company make that happen. Hardage explains that this was only one part of the transition to a new CEO that took place when Kelly took the company's top spot.

Hardage says the company's leaders also looked at how they were spending their time as an executive team and how they were structuring their meetings and sharing information. One result of their work with the MBTI is a more disciplined process for scheduling and focusing their executive meetings.

Inspiration

As an executive, Hardage says that former Southwest president and current president emeritus Colleen Barrett, who was her boss for nineteen years, has been an inspirational person in her life and her career. "She'll forever be my heroine," Hardage says, "and I'll be forever grateful."

Hardage says she also gets inspiration from many other people at Southwest. For example, she singles out "the operations agent that I just met up in Boston. She's already retired. Southwest is her second career. She wanted to work at Southwest so badly that she started working on the ramp. What that means is she's loading bags onto the aircraft. She was able to change jobs later to one that was a little less physically demanding." Hardage says that many of the people who work on Southwest's front lines give her inspiration because they "are very selfless and truly do serve our company."

Southwest has a program called "Winning Spirit" that honors these types of employees. Every month, exemplary employees throughout the organization are nominated by their peers and supervisors. Then, every two months, the nominees who are selected by the Winning Spirit Committee are honored in Dallas by their vice president, are awarded a Winning Spirit Award, and are featured in an article in Southwest's employee magazine, *LUVLines*. CEO Kelly presents the awards.

In a recent article in Southwest's *Spirit* magazine, Kelly wrote that presiding over the Winning Spirit Award ceremonies is one of the "coolest and most rewarding" things that he does in his job as the leader of Southwest. He adds that meeting the company's employees and hearing their stories is his favorite part of the event.

> Whether it is an Employee rushing to the assistance of a victim in an overturned truck, a Reservations Sales Agent preventing a child abduction, or Flight Attendants and their Supervisors sharing hearts with a Customer on the way to identify her son's body, I am touched and humbled by their stories of compassion, courage, and initiative.[11]

Employees respond and engage when their leader speaks in such humane and heartfelt terms such as these.

Employee Recognition

Hardage explains that she draws a tremendous amount of inspiration from the selfless people who have won the Winning Spirit Awards. One of these people is an employee who is going through chemotherapy and is confined to a wheelchair yet continues to arrive at work every day. "That's where the inspiration for me comes from," Hardage says.

To pass that inspiration along to the employees on her team, Hardage models the types of behaviors that she wants to see in her people. This is something that all executives at Southwest try to do. Hardage says, "We definitely try to model it by recognizing those people. We have so many ways of trying to highlight that."

Employee recognition at Southwest Airlines comes in many forms. For example:

- Employees are recognized in Dallas by their bosses and Southwest's CEO with Winning Spirit Awards.
- The stories of outstanding employees are shared with their leaders and peers through Southwest's many employee publications.
- Every week, Gary Kelly records a message to employees in which he give a "shout out" to individuals who have done something special.
- Southwest's Annual Awards Program honors the people in the company who have done extraordinary things throughout the year.
- Southwest publishes a packet of "Good Letters," which contains the customer e-mails and letters that praise the work of the employees at Southwest who went above and beyond the call of duty to make a difference for them during their travel experiences.

Many of these initiatives were started by Barrett while she was the company's president. Driven by her belief in the Golden Rule—treat others as you would want to be treated—and a passion for "servant

---

Servant Leadership

Colleen Barrett is not the first business leader to understand the power of "servant leadership." Many business thinkers refer to Charles F. Haanel as the "Father of Personal Development." The author of the book *The Master Key System* (1919) and other books about improving the human condition, Haanel once wrote, "The first law of success is service. We get what we give, and for this reason we should consider it a great privilege to give."[12]

More recently, leadership guru Stephen R. Covey wrote, "Of necessity, the Age of Wisdom, in my opinion, will follow the Age of Information, where the essence of leadership will be a servant leader." He added, "Service above self is the ethic of all great religions and of all philosophy and psychology that has endured."[13]

For example, Covey points out, legendary scholar and Nobel Peace Prize winner Albert Schweitzer once said, "I know not what your destiny will be, but one thing I know: the only ones among you who will be truly happy are those who have sought and found how to serve."[14] That is the kind of service that lives at the heart of Southwest's business model and in its leadership.

---

leadership," Barrett's influence on Southwest's corporate culture continues to be felt throughout the company today.

INNOVATIONS

Southwest Airlines chairman, president, and CEO Gary Kelly has helped to perpetuate the work of previous leaders at Southwest, including a focus on servant leadership. He has also created many of his own initiatives that have positively affected the company. One of the ways that Kelly has been able to impact Southwest Airlines since taking its reins is by building a stronger foundation for its systems.

Hardage, who works with Kelly every day in Southwest's executive offices, observes, "I think Gary is very logical, so he has definitely put in a lot of structure around how we look at opportunities in the company, because of the speed of change in our world. I think he's put in a lot of discipline in terms of how we're able to capture opportunities and take them to the marketplace as quickly as possible."

Wi-Fi

One example of this is Southwest's recent focus on installing wi-fi capability on many of the company's aircraft. Beginning in February 2009, the airline started testing wi-fi service on four of its airplanes. Customers loved it, so the company has made plans to roll out the Row 44 satellite service throughout its entire fleet of aircraft in early 2010.

In August 2009, Dave Ridley, Southwest Airlines senior vice president of marketing and revenue management, announced:

> We have concluded our testing for in-flight wi-fi and are very happy with both the technical performance of the system and the response of customers who have used it. We are pleased to be continuing with our plans to offer satellite-enabled broadband access through California-based Row 44.[15]

The new wi-fi service aboard Southwest's aircraft allows customers to better use their own wi-fi-enabled devices, such as laptops, iPhones, and smart phones, to access anything from e-mail to streaming video.

Kelly has also led the initiative to install computer charging stations in the gate areas throughout Southwest's system, where passengers can charge their laptops before or after flights. By focusing on these kinds of conveniences for the customer, Southwest responds to their changing needs.

Green Power

Kelly has also backed many environmentally conscious initiatives throughout the company, such as fleetwide advanced avionics, engine washing, and aircraft performance management, which have changed the way the airline impacts the planet. One of these is a "Green Power" initiative that increases efficiency within the company and demonstrates Southwest's environmental commitment.

In August 2009, the Environmental Protection Agency (EPA) updated its National Top Partner lists, highlighting some of America's largest voluntary green power purchasers. The EPA challenged *Fortune* 500 corporations to collectively exceed 10 billion kilowatt-hours of green power purchases—electricity generated from environmentally preferable renewable resources such as wind, solar, geothermal, biogas, biomass, and low-impact hydro—by the end of 2009. The Dallas and Houston operations of Southwest Airlines were ranked number 32 on the EPA's list.

Kelly praised Southwest's efforts: "This was a wonderful initiative by our Green Team, and we are proud to be recognized by the U.S. Environmental Protection Agency. Purchasing green power helps our company become more sustainable, and it helps us in our mission to do the right thing by our planet, our communities, and our people."[16]

According to the EPA, green power has a net zero increase in carbon dioxide emissions, while offering a superior environmental profile compared to traditional power generation sources. Green power purchases also support the development of new renewable energy generation sources nationwide.

Kathleen Hogan, director of the Climate Protection Partnerships Division at the EPA says the "EPA commends our leading partners for their continued commitment to protecting the environment by using green power. By supporting green power, Southwest Airlines is reducing its greenhouse gas emissions, supporting clean energy technologies, and contributing to a clean energy future."[17]

COMMITMENT TO COMMUNICATION

Ginger Hardage describes Gary Kelly as an innovative leader. "I think Gary has put a lot of discipline in how quickly we can bring new innovations to market within the organization." Through process improvement and strategy teams, he has changed the way Southwest changes the world.

While increasing the discipline that is applied to Southwest's innovation process, Kelly also honors the traditions that still work within the company. To do this, Hardage points out, Kelly "devotes an incredible amount of time to communicating with our employees."

For example, every February, Southwest's CEO has conversations with the company's employees in six major employee locations throughout its system. These visits are known as "Messages to the Field." At these events, which were started by Herb Kelleher during

Southwest's early days, Kelly goes out to various sites and delivers a "State of the Company" address to Southwest's people. The mood at these events is much like a pep rally that is attended by hundreds and sometimes thousands of employees.

In 2009, Kelly responded to Southwest's expanding customer base by expanding this traditional program. Deeply committed to communication, Kelly has now added a series of midyear employee conversations to the Messages to the Field program. In late August, he traveled to Los Angeles on Monday, San Diego on Tuesday, and Las Vegas on Wednesday and Thursday.

On each day of these visits, Kelly followed an aggressive schedule. "It starts early in the morning at the flight attendant bases," Hardage points out, "because our flight attendants are coming in and getting on those early morning flights. He starts there at a flight attendant lounge, meeting as many flight attendants as possible, going and having a session with the pilots, spending time with our employees working in the airport in sessions with them." At these events, Kelly answers any questions they might have about the company.

Kelleher and Barrett, while they were CEO and president, respectively, frequently held these types of informal conversations with Southwest's employees. Now that he is president, chairman, and CEO, Kelly carries on the tradition they started, but he has expanded the program to meet the increasing needs of the company's people.

Kelly also uses these events to determine his focus as a leader in the future. When key questions come up again and again during these visits, Kelly realizes their importance and addresses these questions when he next writes in employee publications, speaks in front of employees, or appears in videos on the company's Web site and blog.

SEPTEMBER 11, 2001

Ginger Hardage was working in Southwest's Dallas headquarters when terrorists hijacked four commercial aircraft and crashed two of them into New York's World Trade Center and another into the Pentagon on September 11, 2001. "It was frightening," she remembers. "I think it was frightening for our entire country."

In an interview with *CFO* magazine less than three months after the terrorist attacks of 9/11, Gary Kelly told deputy editor Lori Calabro that he had just walked into his office at Southwest just before 8 A.M. when he heard about the attacks. He was told that an airplane had crashed into the World Trade Center in New York City. When he turned on a television, he said it took him a few moments to understand that the crashed airplane was actually an attack. That was when he immediately started implementing the company's emergency plan and worked to get all of Southwest's airplanes back on the ground. He says, "We have a fleet of 358 airplanes, and at one point there were 150 in the air. It was 10:05 before we got all the planes on the ground and accounted for."[18] When this fact was announced to the employees in Southwest's headquarters, he says that "a cheer went up."

Kelly explains that the primary question he faced that day as chief financial officer for Southwest was, "Do we have cash?" He added that the company was lucky to have had "several hundred million dollars in the bank" on that day, so his attention quickly turned to figuring out what bills the company owed.[19] Then, he focused on determining how long the company might be shut down and when it could resume selling tickets.

Describing that day, Hardage, who was present at the meeting, recalls, "It was very intense."

A Difficult Time

Once the leaders at Southwest had determined that all of their airplanes had landed safely, they turned their attention to all of the company's employees. Hardage explains: "Another thing we had to also do was reassure our employees that layoffs and furloughs would be the last place we would look in this difficult time. I remember Continental Airlines put out a press release on a Saturday about their reductions, their layoffs, and we came in that weekend and immediately got a message out to our employees that Southwest would not be following that course of action." Southwest made sure that its people understood that their jobs were safe.

Meanwhile, over the next few days, Southwest's aircraft sat silent on the runways of Love Field and elsewhere. All air commerce had stopped. No people, goods, or services were being transported on Southwest's airplanes. Everything was put on hold. As people who work directly next to a busy airport, Southwest's people are very used to hearing and seeing airplanes taking off and landing all of the time, and Hardage notes, "To have that eerie quiet for so many days was unsettling." The absence of flights at the airport could be seen every day out of the building's windows.

Two days after the four airliners were hijacked, the U.S. Department of Transportation began to reopen national airspace. Southwest's people saw the occasion as a reason to celebrate. When the first aircraft was scheduled to take off from Love Field for the first flight after 9/11, executives and employees who worked in the company's headquarters lined up on the other side of a high chain-link fence that separates the runways from the employee parking lot. "It was just lined with employees with American flags and singing 'God Bless America' as our first aircraft took off again," Hardage recalls.

Getting Back to Business

Southwest Airlines was the first airline in the United States to begin to advertise its flights after the tragedies on 9/11. The company wanted to let people know that the airline was ready for them.

In her October 1, 2002, article for *Boards* magazine, Sara Minogue wrote about the occasion. She explains that Southwest's decision to become the first airline to advertise after the terrorist attacks was a momentous occasion that made headlines around the country. One week later, Southwest launched its "Compassion" advertising campaign. Minogue explains, "GSD&M creative directors Brent Ladd and Steve Miller got the call for the ads on Friday, September 14th. . . . The spots aired that Wednesday, vowing to 'Keep America Flying.' "[20] The tone of these ads demonstrated the deep emotional commitment that Southwest's leaders felt toward both their employees and their passengers.

The "Compassion" campaign was made up of five advertisements that were short and to the point. They were also patriotic. Each of the TV advertisements showed employees of Southwest Airlines who were committed to their work for the company. According to Minogue, Colleen Barrett, who was Southwest's president and chief operating officer at the time, spent the weekend in her own home recording the voiceover that was used on the commercials.

In her *Boards* article, Minogue writes:

> Cynthia Hill [Southwest's director of advertising] believes the ads worked because "those words were the first message that went out to our employees. They were from the heart of the company. [Barrett] considered them like public announcements. We were saying we felt united as an airline."[21]

Love and compassion were already built into Southwest's corporate values, so these emotions came naturally to the company. During its most difficult times, they helped to bring the company's people and passengers back together again.

In its first advertisements after 9/11, Southwest Airlines focused on its customers with compassion and empathy. Executives at Southwest wanted to let their customers know that the airline was there for them when they were ready to fly.

Hardage, who was director of public relations at the time, explains, "We knew a lot of people would be afraid to fly." Instead of pushing its customers to hurry back to the airline, Southwest told passengers, when you are ready, we're here for you.

TOUGH TIMES

The months following 9/11 were difficult times, but the economic recession at the end of 2008 and through 2009 also presented the company with many challenges. Interviewed in 2009, Ginger Hardage said, "We're in an economic crisis now that's far greater than we experienced after 9/11. Of course, many of our employees are asking about furloughs, and we can't promise that can never happen. I don't think anyone knows how bad business could get, but that will be one of the last things we will do."

On April 16, 2009, to help reduce the company's workforce and cut costs without laying off its employees, Southwest Airlines announced that it was offering voluntary buyout packages to all employees who were willing to retire early. It also announced a hiring freeze. In addition, CEO Gary Kelly announced that pay for top officers and senior management was frozen.

During the duration of the voluntary buyout program, which lasted for two months, 1,400 employees voluntarily separated from the company, taking advantage of the company's offer, which included severance pay that was based on their length of service, and many other benefits.

The company announced the voluntary buyout program on the same day that it announced its first-quarter losses for 2009. Southwest reportedly lost $91 million, or 12 cents a share, compared with earnings of $34 million, or 5 cents a share, in the first quarter of the previous year. In his statement to the press, Kelly said, "A rapid weakening in passenger demand, particularly among business travelers, led to our first quarter net loss."[22]

Most of the posted loss for the first quarter of 2009—$71 million—"was attributed to Southwest's fuel-hedge portfolio. Hedges are contracts locked in far in advance to purchase jet fuel," wrote *Philadelphia Inquirer* staff writer Linda Loyd.[23]

Fuel hedging can be a gamble. For Southwest, the results were mixed. When the price of oil peaked at $147 per barrel in July 2008, Southwest's fuel-hedging contracts helped the company save millions of dollars. But the price of oil fell steeply in the beginning of 2009. At the time of the announced first-quarter loss, the price of oil was down to around $50 per barrel.

CORPORATE CULTS

In 2000, Dallas Baptist University professor of management Dave Arnott published his book *Corporate Cults: The Insidious Lure of the All-Consuming Organization*, which cited Southwest Airlines, 3M, and Microsoft as examples of companies that exhibit "cultish" corporate cultures. According to Arnott, employees are "culted" when what they do defines who they are: "People should find more value in who they are and less value in what they do. Employees to whom work has become too important have allowed their workplace to become their own corporate cult."[24]

On the first pages of his book, Arnott presents Southwest Airlines as his first example of a company that could be defined as a corporate cult. Ginger Hardage says that she has heard this accusation before, but laughs at the comparison. In her opinion, "If a cult is trying to deliver great customer service and taking care of your employees and being people-centric, well, then I don't mind!" She adds, "I find it humorous."

SAFETY

Safety is one of Southwest's primary concerns as an airline. Although it recently came under fire for the conduct of one of its vendors, which was caught using unauthorized parts on Southwest's aircraft—parts the airline promptly replaced—Southwest Airlines has an exemplary safety record.

Every year, Southwest carries between 90 million and 100 million people on its aircraft. Over all of the time the company has been in operation, only one person has died as a result of a problem at Southwest. "We have only had one fatality in our thirty-eight-year history," Hardage confirms. "One of our aircraft, in a snowstorm ran off the end of a runway in Chicago Midway [Airport] and struck a car. A six-year-old in that car was killed." Despite that tragedy, Hardage says she remains proud of her company's safety record, which is one of the best safety records of all the airlines in the world.

THE GREATEST IMPACT

Looking back at Southwest Airlines' four-decade history, Ginger Hardage sees a company that has achieved many important milestones. She explains that the way her company has positively affected the lives of so many people is the one thing that makes it a corporation that has truly changed the world for the better: "It goes back to the basics of really changing air travel in America and being a model for corporate governance and the way we conduct ourselves and interact with our customers and our employees.

"The other thing I look at is how many lives the company has changed; how many of our employees have educated their families, or bought a house, or retired in the mountains where they wanted to, because of the career that Southwest Airlines gave them, or how many of our customers have been able to grow their business. We hear all the time from people who have been able to carry on long-term relationships when they were in different cities. I think the greatest impact will be the way it helped change people's lives for the better."

Appendix

Southwest Airlines Timeline

1971   Through the hard work of founders Rollin King and Herb Kelleher, Southwest Airlines incorporates. With four Boeing 737s, Southwest Airlines flies its first flights between Dallas, Houston, and San Antonio. Lamar Muse is president of the company.

1972   Service in Houston is transferred from Houston Intercontinental Airport to Hobby Airport. When the company has trouble making its payroll, rather than laying off its employees it sells its fourth aircraft to pay its people. Since airplanes make money in the air and not on the ground, the idea of the "ten-minute turn" is born; Southwest's fast turns make it an industry leader and a role model for airline productivity.

1973   For the first time in the company's short history, Southwest Airlines has a profitable year. The company files with the Texas Aeronautics Commission to extend its service into the Rio Grande Valley. It also introduces RUSH Cargo service, which offers same-day airport cargo delivery.

1974   Southwest flies its millionth passenger. The company adds two new boarding gates and departure lounges to the terminal at Houston's Hobby Airport at a cost of $400,000.

1975   The Texas Aeronautics Commission grants Southwest permission to fly passengers to the Rio Grande Valley via the Harlingen Airport; the company begins four roundtrips each business day. Southwest adds a fifth Boeing 737 to its fleet.

1976   A sixth Boeing 737 is added to Southwest's fleet. More than a million and a half passengers fly on the company's flights. Operations begin to Austin, Corpus Christi, El Paso, Lubbock, and Midland/Odessa.

1977   The five millionth passenger is carried by Southwest Airlines. Southwest's stock is listed on the New York Stock Exchange; the symbol for Southwest is LUV.

1978   Kelleher steps in as interim president, CEO, and chairman of the board of Southwest Airlines when Muse steps down as president. Southwest Airlines aircraft N52SW is christened the *Herbert D. Kelleher* in honor if the airline's cofounder. Later in the year, Howard D. Putnam is unanimously elected as Southwest's president and CEO; Kelleher stays on as the company's permanent chairman of the board. On December 12, Southwest begins to serve Amarillo.

1979   To add convenience and speed to its boarding process, Southwest introduces self-ticketing machines in ten cities. The airline also begins service to New Orleans from Dallas, making it the first city outside of Texas to be served by Southwest Airlines. A federal law restricting interstate travel from Dallas's Love Field—the Wright Amendment—is enacted.

1980   The twenty-second Boeing 737 is added to Southwest's fleet, the first to be completely owned by Southwest Airlines. The aircraft is christened the *Rollin W. King* in honor of the company's cofounder.

1981   Recruited by the board of directors at Braniff International Airlines, Putnam leaves his position as CEO at Southwest Airlines to become the CEO at Braniff, where he takes the financially struggling airline through and out of Chapter 11 bankruptcy. Southwest Airlines celebrates its ten-year anniversary as a carrier. The company now employees 2,129 employees and operates twenty-seven aircraft.

1982   Kelleher becomes Southwest's permanent president, CEO, and chairman of the board. The airline begins flights to San Francisco, Los Angeles, San Diego, Las Vegas, Kansas City, and Phoenix.

1983   The company buys three more 737-200s, schedules more flights than ever, flies more than 9,500,000 passengers, and begins to serve Denver's Stapleton Airport.

1984   Southwest Airlines continues to grow its capacity and profits thanks to positive relations with its labor unions. The airline begins to serve Little Rock, Arkansas. Southwest celebrates the eighty-first anniversary of the Wright Brothers' first flight by introducing the first 737-300, which is christened the *Spirit of Kitty Hawk* in honor of the occasion.

1985   Southwest begins service in Ontario, California; in St. Louis; and at Chicago's Midway Airport. The Ronald McDonald House is named as Southwest Airlines' primary charity. Southwest launches the "Just Say When" campaign, which helps to establish the company as the most convenient point-to-point carrier in the United States. The company also acquires Muse Air from Lamar Muse, Southwest's first president. Muse Air is operated by

Southwest as a wholly owned subsidiary. The company is renamed TranStar Airlines.

1986   Southwest starts its Fun Fares program, which leads to more than 13 million passengers flying on the company's aircraft. A new multimillion-dollar Training Center for Flight Crews is opened. Southwest begins service to Nashville; operational issues cause it to stop flights to Denver. After fifteen years in business, the company now has seventy-nine aircraft and 5,819 employees.

1987   Southwest begins its "Company Plane" advertising campaign to appeal to more business travelers. It also introduces its first frequent flyer program, the Company Club, which will eventually become the Rapid Rewards program. While its competitors' programs base their rewards on accrued mileage, Southwest's program awards passengers for the number of trips they take. Southwest sells off TranStar Airlines because the company's business plan and operations do not coincide with Southwest's corporate strategy.

1988   Southwest Airlines and SeaWorld of Texas work together to promote Texas as a major tourist attraction through a campaign called "New Friends." In honor of the partnership, Southwest becomes SeaWorld of Texas's official airline. *Shamu One*, a Boeing 737 painted like Shamu the killer whale, is unveiled. Later in the year, Southwest becomes the official airline of SeaWorld of California. The airline wins its first monthly Triple Crown for Best On-Time Record, Best Baggage Handling, and Fewest Customer Complaints from the Department of Transportation (DOT) Air Travel Consumer Reports.

1989   Southwest Airlines reaches the milestone of $1 billion in revenue. In honor of its partnerships with SeaWorld Texas and SeaWorld California, Southwest launches *Shamu Two*, a second aircraft painted like a killer whale. The airline also begins service from Oakland and Indianapolis. CBS News airs a profile of Southwest Airlines on its popular news program *60 Minutes*.

1990   Southwest creates its unique Corporate Culture Committee to help the company extend its breakthrough corporate culture among employees. The company introduces the 737-500 into airline service. A new Southwest terminal—Terminal 4—is opened in Phoenix. The airline begins to serve Burbank, California, and Reno, Nevada. To mark the company's twentieth anniversary the following year, Southwest launches its anniversary "flagship" aircraft with *Lone Star One*.

1991   To celebrate its twentieth anniversary, Southwest holds simultaneous birthday parties at all thirty-two of its stations across the country on June 18. The company also starts service to

Sacramento, California. To support U.S. troops serving in the first Gulf War, Southwest employees launch a program called "LUV-GRAMS—Send Your Heart to Saudi." By the end of the year, Southwest Airlines employs 9,778 people and flies 124 aircraft.

1992   Southwest Airlines wins the first annual airline Triple Crown from the Department of Transportation (DOT) for best on-time performance, best baggage handling, and fewest customer complaints of all major airlines. Southwest begins to serve Ohio with flights to and from Cleveland and Columbus.

When a conflict arises between Stevens Aviation and Southwest Airlines over which company has the right to use the slogan "Just Plane Smart," Southwest's CEO Kelleher and Stevens Aviation's chairman Kurt Herwald decide to settle the argument by arm wrestling. The fun event is called "The Malice in Dallas." With a cigarette dangling from his lips, Kelleher loses the match, but Herwald gives Southwest the right to use the slogan. All proceeds from the arm wrestling event go to local charities.

1993   Southwest Airlines begins service to the East Coast by opening a station at Baltimore/Washington International Airport. The

In March 1992, Southwest's founder Herb Kelleher (with cigarette) and Stevens Aviation chairman Kurt Herwald arm wrestle for the rights to use the slogan "Just Plane Smart." Although Kelleher lost the match, Herwald decided to allow Southwest to keep using the slogan, and the event raised $15,000 for charity. (Courtesy Southwest Airlines.)

airline also begins service to Louisville, Kentucky. To celebrate Valentine's Day, Southwest Airlines awards the first Heroes of the Heart Awards, which recognize the company's employees and work groups that are often out of the public eye but are vital to Southwest's success.

After fifty days of negotiations, on December 31, Southwest Airlines acquires Morris Air, a carrier based in Salt Lake City, paying about $129 million in a stock swap. Morris Air, about an eighth of the size of Southwest Airlines, was started by June M. Morris, a former travel agent who built her company around Southwest's low-fares, no-frills business model. Like Southwest, Morris Air also used only Boeing 737 jets. Southwest's purchase of Morris Air showed its competitors that it was emerging as more of a national company than its regional name implies. The purchase added fourteen cities in the northwest and western United States to its schedule. Southwest also gained twenty-one planes in the deal. The deal pushed Southwest's stock up $2, putting it at $36 in trading on the New York Stock Exchange. The deal to buy Morris was Southwest's second acquisition (the first was Muse Air in 1985).

1994   Southwest Airlines introduces ticketless travel in four cities. The aircraft *Arizona One* is unveiled. With the integration of Morris Air, Southwest begins service in seven new cities, including Seattle, Spokane, Portland, Salt Lake City, and Boise in the Pacific Northwest, and Orange County and Tucson in the Southwest. To celebrate the joining of the two airlines, Southwest holds a symbolic Las Vegas wedding ceremony at the Graceland Wedding Chapel.

1995   After the ticketless travel program proves successful in its initial markets, the program is made available throughout the entire Southwest Airlines system in January. In honor of its California passengers, Southwest unveils its aircraft *California One* in Sacramento. Throughout the year, the plane tours the state. Omaha is now served by Southwest Airlines. For the fourth year in a row, Southwest Airlines wins the coveted annual airline Triple Crown. To help passengers book their flights online, the company starts the "Southwest Airlines Home Gate," which will eventually turn into the company's current Web site, www.southwest.com.

1996   In January, Southwest Airlines begins service to Tampa Bay and Ft. Lauderdale, Florida; in April, Southwest's service to Florida is also expanded to Orlando. To celebrate its twenty-fifth anniversary, the company launches *Silver One*. For the first time, Ticketless Travel Online becomes available on www.southwest.com. Southwest's frequent flyer program is renamed Rapid Rewards.

In October, Southwest begins service to Providence, Rhode Island. By the end of the year, Southwest has 22,944 employees and flies 243 airplanes.

1997   The fiftieth city is added to Southwest's schedule when it begins service to Jacksonville, Florida; in August, Jackson, Mississippi, becomes the fifty-first. To honor the employees at Southwest who helped the company win the annual airline Triple Crown for five years in a row, the airline launches the *Triple Crown One* aircraft; the Triple Crown trophy is subsequently retired. To expand its service to local communities in the cities it serves, Southwest introduces its Adopt-a-Pilot Community Service program, in which Southwest's pilots adopt a fifth-grade class somewhere in the Southwest system. The company also celebrates the passage of the Shelby Amendment, which modifies the Wright Amendment, allowing Southwest to fly nonstop flights from Love Field in Dallas to Mississippi, Alabama, and Kansas. In December, Southwest receives and puts into service its first Boeing 737-700.

1998   On June 7, Southwest begins service to Manchester, New Hampshire. The airline also moves into new facilities in St. Louis, Sacramento, and Ontario. In addition, Southwest Airlines begins to experiment with its first transcontinental flights over the busy Thanksgiving travel weekend.

1999   On March 1, Southwest Airlines begins to offer twelve flights a day from Long Island at MacArthur Airport in Islip, New York, to Baltimore/Washington, Chicago, Nashville, and Tampa. On May 23, all of the airline's Austin services move from Austin's Mueller Airport to the Austin-Bergstrom International Airport. In honor of the state of Nevada, Southwest unveils *Nevada One*. On June 6, the airline starts to fly in and out of Raleigh-Durham International Airport in North Carolina. In August, Southwest puts its three-hundredth aircraft into service. On October 31, the company begins to serve Bradley International Airport in Hartford, Connecticut.

2000   To help company's travel managers book and track the trips of their people that are booked via www.southwest.com, Southwest on May 1 introduces a business tool called "SWABIZ." On May 5, the company holds the first annual Phoenix LUV Classic Golf Tournament and Party; all money raised by the tournament goes to the Ronald McDonald House. Three days later, Southwest begins service to Albany International Airport in New York. On October 8, Southwest opens its service to the Buffalo-Niagara International Airport. As a salute to the state of New Mexico, Southwest presents its tenth specialty aircraft to the public: *New Mexico One*.

2001   On January 22, Southwest Airlines begins to fly passengers to West Palm Beach, Florida. To celebrate its thirtieth anniversary as an airline, Southwest unveils the *Spirit One* aircraft. The company also orders all of its new Boeing 737s to be painted with the new "Canyon Blue" exterior color scheme; all new aircraft deliveries would also feature all-leather seats (eventually the entire existing fleet would be retrofitted to meet the new standards). James F. Parker becomes Southwest Airlines' new CEO, and Colleen Barrett is named Southwest Airlines' president, becoming the first female president of a major airline.

On September 11, al-Qaeda terrorists hijack four airplanes belonging to other airlines. Two of the commercial airliners are crashed into the Twin Towers of the World Trade Center in New York City; a third plane is crashed into the headquarters of the U.S. Department of Defense at the Pentagon in Arlington, Virginia, outside of Washington, D.C.; and the fourth, which was heading toward Washington, D.C., crashes into a field near Shanksville, Pennsylvania, after several passengers and crew members tried to regain control of the plane. After the attacks, U.S. air travel is temporarily suspended. The public's subsequent fear of flying leads to an economic freefall for the airline industry, and the airline industry suffers record economic losses. Other

To mark its thirtieth anniversary as an airline, Southwest unveiled its new color scheme. (Courtesy Southwest Airlines.)

airlines lay off nearly one hundred thousand employees, and 20 percent of the U.S. commercial aircraft fleet is grounded. Despite the devastation to the airline industry—which had already been suffering from a steep economic decline thanks to a recession—Southwest refuses to lay off a single employee. Within a month of the attacks, Southwest begins service to Norfolk, Virginia, on October 8. By the end of the year, Southwest Airlines is flying 344 aircraft and employs 29,274 people.

2002   In an effort to reduce the amount of time its customers spend waiting in line and to improve the customer experience in airports following the 9/11 terrorist attacks, Southwest revamps its boarding process. The airline starts to retire its reusable plastic boarding cards and, with the help of IBM, installs nearly 250 self-service check-in kiosks at many of the airports it serves. In addition, Southwest's new corporate logo is unveiled.

2003   Southwest begins to install performance-enhancing blended winglets on its planes, a technological breakthrough in aviation engineering that extends the airplane's range, saves fuel, lowers engine maintenance costs, and reduces takeoff noise; the current fleet is retrofitted with the blended winglets, and all future 737-700s would be delivered with them. *Air Transport World* magazine selects Southwest as its Airline of the Year. At *InsideFlyer* magazine's fifteenth annual Freddie Awards, Southwest's Rapid Rewards program is honored with the first place award for Best Customer Service, Best Bonus Promotion, and Best Award Redemption. A&E television network announces it will partner with Southwest Airlines to film a real-life, behind-the-scenes look at the daily drama of the people who work in the commercial airline industry.

2004   Southwest Airlines makes the announcement that it has made a profit for thirty-one years in a row. The airline begins to offer passengers the option of obtaining their boarding passes through www.southwest.com; this new feature on the company's Web site allows customers to go directly to the departure gate without having to stop at a ticket counter, Skycap, or self-service kiosk. On May 9, Southwest begins serving Philadelphia International Airport, the sixtieth airport served by Southwest; the company now flies 2,800 daily flights to fifty-nine cities. In July, Parker retires as Southwest's CEO and is replaced by Southwest's former controller and CFO Gary Kelly. In November, Kelly announces that Southwest Airlines is no longer "neutral" on the Wright Amendment and begins a new legal battle to have the amendment repealed.

2005   This is the thirty-second consecutive year of profitability for Southwest Airlines—no other airline had previously reached this milestone. Southwest introduces a new code-share agreement with ATA Airlines, providing its customers with access to more cities with more connections; the deal with ATA brings in nearly $50 million in annual revenue for Southwest. The company also announces the introduction of *DING!*, the first-ever direct link to customers' computers and mobile devices that delivers live updates on the most recent airfare deals and promotions. In addition, Southwest starts its "southwestgiftcard" program, which allows customers to give the gift of flight.

The airline begins to fly to Pittsburgh, Pennsylvania, and to Ft. Myers, Florida; Southwest now flies more than 3,000 daily flights. To help customers and employees support its efforts to repeal the Wright Amendment, Southwest Airlines launches the www.setlovefree.com Web site. Missouri is removed from the legal boundaries of the Wright Amendment. Two new specialty aircraft are unveiled: *Maryland One*, honoring the state of Maryland, and *Slam Dunk One*, honoring Southwest's status as the "official airline" of the National Basketball Association. Online check-in is extended to twenty-four hours prior to departure at www.southwest.com.

On December 8, the flight crew on one of Southwest's 737-700s is unable to stop the airplane after landing on the runway at Chicago's Midway Airport. The aircraft breaks through the airport's barrier fence and rolls onto a nearby street where it strikes two vehicles. The crash causes fatal injuries to a six-year-old boy in one of the vehicles; nobody on board the airplane is seriously injured. This is Southwest's first fatal accident and the first serious accident involving a 737-700.

2006   Southwest announces that flights have been reintroduced to Denver, and service begins to the Dulles International Airport in Washington, D.C. The airline receives the rank of number one in customer satisfaction for 2006. Twenty-six Boeing 737-700s are added to Southwest's fleet, which help it fly nearly 3,200 flights every day.

After twenty-seven years of legal wrangling, the Wright Amendment is removed. Although some restrictions remain, the amendment will be completely repealed in 2014, at which time Southwest will be allowed to have nonstop service from Dallas to any airport the airline serves.

2007   Southwest Airlines signs a ten-year contract with Galileo to make low fares available to all Galileo-connected travel agencies in North America. Southwest returns to San Francisco International Airport in the summer and expands with an eighth crew base, located in Las Vegas. In response to customer feedback, Southwest keeps its open-seating policy but adopts a new boarding procedure to make the process quicker. Southwest adds a new

Business Select fare for its most frequent business flyers. Southwest Airlines is voted "Overall Best Airline" in the United States by Frost & Sullivan's CEO Leadership Forum. According to PhoCusWright, in 2007 Southwest.com is the number one airline Web site for online revenue. *Travel and Leisure* magazine ranks Southwest Airlines fourth among the Top Domestic Carriers, and Southwest receives the distinctive honor of being named the Best Domestic Airline by *Travel Weekly* magazine. In April, the Port of Portland presents Southwest Airlines with an Environmental Excellence Award in recognition of its exemplary effort in the category of Environmental Innovation. Southwest Airlines is included in *Hispanic Business* magazine's Top 60 Diversity Elite for 2007.

2008 Year-end results for 2008 mark Southwest Airlines' thirty-fifth consecutive year of profitability. It is now the United States' most successful low-fare, high-frequency, point-to-point carrier, operating more than 3,300 daily flights, becoming the largest U.S. carrier based on domestic departures as of September 30. There are more than 35,000 Southwest employees throughout its system. For the year, Southwest flies 101.9 million passengers to sixty-six cities in thirty-three states and moves 225 million pounds of cargo. In the process, it serves 55.2 million cans of soda, juices, and water; 12.4 million alcoholic beverages; 9.8 million bags of pretzels; 90.8 million bags of peanuts; 9 million snack boxes; and 32 million other snacks.

For the twelfth consecutive year, *Fortune* recognizes Southwest Airlines in its annual survey of corporate reputations: Southwest Airlines is the only airline to make the Top 20 list and also earn the top spot on the Most Admired Airline list. In October, *Nuts About Southwest* is awarded "Best Blog" for the second year in a row by *PR News*.

2009 After several months of testing, Southwest Airlines begins to install wi-fi Internet service on many of its aircraft. According to Comscore Mediametrix, in January 2009, Southwest.com is the fourth largest travel site and the largest airline site in terms of unique visitors. In the first quarter of 2009, about 77 percent of Southwest's customers check in online or at a kiosk. In March, Southwest Airlines is ranked number three on CampusGrotto's list of Best College Internship Programs. When Southwest begins service to LaGuardia Airport on June 28, it is the first time that the airline has serviced New York City directly. In early August, Southwest attempts to acquire Frontier Airlines, but its bid of more than $170 million is not selected; Republic Airways acquires the company instead. On August 17, Southwest Airlines begins service to the E Terminal at Boston Logan Airport. On November 1,

This is the company logo used by Southwest Airlines in 2009. (Courtesy Southwest Airlines.)

Southwest begins service to Milwaukee, bringing the total number of cities served by the airline to sixty-eight. Southwest now flies 544 aircraft, all Boeing 737 jets, to thirty-three states.

2010 Southwest adds nonstop service from St. Louis to Boston and Minneapolis in January. It also begins new nonstop service between Denver and Boston Logan, Denver and Spokane, and Denver and Reno/Tahoe. Southwest Airlines and Internet wi-fi service provider Row 44 roll out wi-fi services on all of Southwest's aircraft. The airline pursues its first international flights using its own airplanes by working to form partnerships with other airlines that fly to Mexico and Canada. Southwest now serves sixty-eight cities in thirty-five states. Southwest declares 134th consecutive quarterly dividend.

Notes

CHAPTER 1

1. James O'Toole and Edward E. Lawler III, *The New American Workplace* (New York: Palgrave Macmillan, 2006).

2. Bob Johansen, *Leaders Make the Future* (San Francisco: Berrett-Koehler, 2009).

3. "Southwest Cares: Doing the Right Thing—Mission and Vision," available at http://www.southwest.com/about_swa/southwest_cares/mission_and_vision.html.

4. "Southwest Cares: Doing the Right Thing—Our Planet," available at http://www.southwest.com/about_swa/southwest_cares/our_planet.html.

5. "We Weren't Just Airborne Yesterday: Time Flies When You're Having Fun," available at http://www.southwest.com/about_swa/airborne.html.

CHAPTER 2

1. Quoted in Joseph Guinto, "Rollin On," *Southwest Airlines Spirit*, June 2006, 135.

2. Terry Maxon, "Southwest Founder: Hit and Myth," interview with Rollin King, *Dallas Morning News*, May 16, 2007.

3. Kevin Freiberg and Jackie Freiberg, *Nuts! Southwest Airlines' Crazy Recipe for Business and Personal Success* (New York: Broadway Books, 1998), 15.

4. Maxon, "Southwest Founder."

5. "Executive Profile: Rollin W. King," *BusinessWeek*, available at http://investing.businessweek.com/businessweek/research/stocks/people/person.asp?personId=632020&ric=LUV.

6. Katrina Brooker and Alynda Wheat, "The Chairman of the Board Looks Back," *Fortune*, May 28, 2001, available at http://money.cnn.com/magazines/fortune/fortune_archive/2001/05/28/303852/index.htm.

7. Brooker and Wheat, "Chairman of the Board Looks Back," available at http://money.cnn.com/magazines/fortune/fortune_archive/2001/05/28/303852/index.htm.

8. Mukul Pandya and Robbie Shell, *Lasting Leadership: Lessons from the Twenty-Five Most Influential Business People of Our Times* (Upper Saddle River, NJ: Wharton School Publishing, 2004), 23.

9. Pandya and Shell, *Lasting Leadership*, 23.

10. Pandya and Shell, *Lasting Leadership*, 24.

11. "Lamar Muse, 86, Helped Southwest Airlines Ascend," *Washington Post*, February 8, 2007, available at http://www.washingtonpost.com/wp-dyn/content/article/2007/02/07/AR2007020702275.html.

12. Pandya and Shell, *Lasting Leadership*, 24.

13. "Lamar Muse," *Washington Post*.

14. "Southwest Airlines' Colleen Barrett Flies High on Fuel Hedging and 'Servant Leadership,'" Knowledge@Wharton, July 9, 2008, available at http://knowledge.wharton.upenn.edu/article.cfm?articleid=2006. Subsequent Barrett quotes from this source.

15. Adam Bryant. "James Parker: CEO, Southwest Airlines" *Newsweek*, (December 31, 2001).

16. Aude Lagorce, "Southwest CEO Lands in Hot Seat," *Forbes*, March 29, 2004, available at http://www.forbes.com/2004/03/29/cx_al_0329southwest.html.

17. "Parker Steps Down as Southwest CEO, Kelly Tapped as Successor," *Business Travel News*, July 15, 2004, available at http://www.btnonline.com/businesstravelnews/headlines/article_display.jsp?vnu_content_id=1000578580.

18. James F. Parker, *Do the Right Thing: How Dedicated Employees Create Loyal Customers and Large Profits* (Upper Saddle River, NJ: Wharton School Publishing, 2007).

19. Shephard Group, "Southwest Airlines releases 2Q09 earnings," available at http://www.shephard.co.uk/news/3403/.

20. Douglas Mcintyre, "Continental Loses $213 Million, Will Cut 1,700 Jobs, Raise Fares," *DailyFinance*, July 21, 2001, available at http://www.dailyfinance.com/2009/07/21/continental-loses-213-million-will-cut-1-700-jobs-raise-fares.

CHAPTER 3

1. "'Warrior Spirit with a Servant's Heart': SWA's Thriving Culture of Service," Knowledge@W.P. Carey, May 24, 2006, available at http://knowledge.wpcarey.asu.edu/article.cfm?articleid=1253.

2. Jill Rose, "Fly Right," *American Executive*, December 31, 2007, available at http://www.americanexecutive.com/index.php?option=com_content&task=view&id=6124.

CHAPTER 4

1. Charles S. Jacobs, *Management Rewired: Why Feedback Doesn't Work and Other Surprising Lessons from the Latest Brain Science* (New York: Portfolio, 2009).

2. Herb Kelleher, "Building a People-Focused Culture," presentation to HSM Global, October 14, 2008, available at http://hsm.typepad.com/inspiringideas/management. Subsequent Kelleher quotes from this source.

3. John H. Zenger and Joseph Folkman, *The Extraordinary Leader: Turning Good Managers into Great Leaders* (New York: McGraw-Hill, 2009), 253.

4. Zenger and Folkman, *Extraordinary Leader*, 253.

5. W. Chan Kim and Renée Mauborgne, *Blue Ocean Strategy: How to Create Uncontested Market Space and Make the Competition Irrelevant* (Boston: Harvard Business School Press, 2005).

6. Kim and Mauborgne, *Blue Ocean Strategy*, 38.

7. Pamela Bilbrey and Brian Jones. *Ordinary Greatness: It's Where You Least Expect It . . . Everywhere* (Hoboken, NJ: John Wiley & Sons, 2009).

8. John Gerzema and Ed Lebar, *The Brand Bubble: The Looming Crisis in Brand Value and How to Avoid It* (San Francisco: Jossey-Bass, 2008), 42–43.

9. Gerzema and Lebar, *Brand Bubble*, 43.

10. Gerzema and Lebar, *Brand Bubble*, 124–25.

11. "Webcast Archive." Smithsonian National Air and Space Museum, July 19, 2009, available at http://www.nasm.si.edu/webcasts/archive.cfm (accessed Sept. 18, 2009).

12. James O'Toole and Edward E. Lawler III, *The New American Workplace* (New York: Palgrave Macmillan, 2006), 165.

13. O'Toole and Lawler, *New American Workplace*, 165.

14. J. C. Larreche, *The Momentum Effect: How to Ignite Exceptional Growth* (Upper Saddle River, NJ: Wharton School Publishing, 2008), 94–95.

15. Larreche, *Momentum Effect*, 95.

16. Larreche, *Momentum Effect*, 95.

17. Larreche, *Momentum Effect*, 236.

18. David Sirota, Louis A. Mischkind, and Michael Irwin Meltzer, *The Enthusiastic Employee: How Companies Profit by Giving Workers What They Want* (Upper Saddle River, NJ: Wharton School Publishing, 2005).

19. Lester Thurow, "Worst News on Layoffs Lies Ahead," *USA Today*, March 22, 2001, quoted in Sirota, Mischkind, and Meltzer, *Enthusiastic Employee*.

20. Sirota, Mischkind, and Meltzer, *Enthusiastic Employee*, 65.

21. Parker, James. "Where Layoffs Are a Last Resort." *BusinessWeek* Online, October 8, 2001, available at http://www.businessweek.com/magazine/content/01_41/b3752712.htm (accessed Sept. 19, 2009).

CHAPTER 6

1. "Southwest Airlines Historical Advertising Gallery," available at http://www.southwest.com/about_swa/netads.html.

2. Sara Minogue, "Southwest Airlines," *Boards*, October 1, 2002, available at http://www.boardsmag.com/articles/magazine/20021001/south.html.

3. Bill Taylor, "GSD&M, Southwest Airlines, and the Power of Ideas," September 5, 2007, available at http://blogs.harvardbusiness.org/taylor/2007/09/gsdm_southwest_airlines_and_th.html.

4. Taylor, "GSD&M."

5. Reuters, "Southwest Plans Buyouts after a Big Quarterly Loss," *New York Times*, April 17, 2009.

6. Matthew E. May, *In Pursuit of Elegance: Why the Best Ideas Have Something Missing* (New York: Broadway Books, 2009).

7. Bloomberg News, "Southwest Brings Back Honey-Roasted Peanuts," *Dallas Morning News*, April 10, 2007.

8. Mya Frazier, "Southwest Airlines: A Marketing 50 Case Study," *Advertising Age*, November 17, 2008, available at http://adage.com/article?article_id=132428.

9. Jonah Lehrer, *How We Decide* (New York: Houghton Mifflin Harcourt, 2009), 183–84.

10. Lehrer, *How We Decide*, 184.

11. James L. Heskett, W. Earl Sasser Jr., and Leonard A. Schlesinger, *The Service Profit Chain: How Leading Companies Link Profit and Growth to Loyalty, Satisfaction, and Value* (New York: Free Press, 1997), 239.

12. Heskett, Sasser, and Schlesinger, *Service Profit Chain*, 239.

13. Southwest Airlines, "Policy Concerning Harassment, Sexual Harassment or Discrimination" July 2008, available at http://www.southwest.com/about_swa/southwest_cares/harassment_policy.pdf.

14. Southwest Airlines, "Supplier Information," available at http://www.southwest.com/about_swa/supplier_information.html.

15. Mary Miller, "Business Ethics 100 Best Corporate Citizens 2002," *Business Ethics*, March/April 2002, available at http://www.thecro.com/be_citizens2002.

16. Miller, "Business Ethics," March/April 2002, available at http://www.thecro.com/be_citizens2002.

17. "Southwest Airlines and the FAA revolutionize the skies," *eTurbo News*, June 19, 2008, available at http://www.eturbonews.com/3192/southwest-airlines-and-faa-revolutionize-skie.

18. Mark Twain, *The Innocents Abroad* (Hartford, CT: American Publishing Co., 1869).

CHAPTER 7

1. Randy Rickard, interview by Steve Heaser, "One Man's Dream," *Nuts About Southwest*, May 20, 2009, available at http://www.blogsouthwest.com/taxonomy/term/722/all. Subsequent Rickard quotes from this source.

2. Boeing Web site, "The Boeing Next-Generation 737 Family," available at http://www.boeing.com/commercial/737family/background.html.

3. Boeing, "The Secret Behind High Profits at Low-Fare Airlines," press release, June 14, 2002, available at http://www.boeing.com/commercial/news/feature/profit.html.

4. Robert Hewson, *The Vital Guide to Commercial Aircraft and Airliners* (Shrewsbury, England: Airlife, 1994).

5. Boeing, "Secret Behind High Profits."

6. Boeing, "Secret Behind High Profits."

CHAPTER 8

1. Justin Martin, "Dancing with Elephants," *Fortune Small Business*, October 1, 2004, available at http://money.cnn.com/magazines/fsb/fsb_archive/2004/10/01/8187270/index.htm.

2. Martin, "Dancing with Elephants."

3. James L. Heskett, W. Earl Sasser Jr., and Leonard A. Schlesinger, *The Service Profit Chain: How Leading Companies Link Profit and Growth to Loyalty, Satisfaction, and Value* (New York: Free Press, 1997), 116.

CHAPTER 9

1. Http://www.youtube.com/watch?v=ivjybzdXVmI.

2. © David Holmes. Used with permission.

3. Heather Poole, "Galley Gossip: Flight Attendant of the Month—David Holmes," *Gadling*, May 8, 2009, available at http://www.gadling.com/2009/05/08/galley-gossip-flight-attendant-of-the-month-david-holmes-s/.

4. Http://www.blogsouthwest.com/blog/i-blogged-you-flamed-we-changed.

5. Jessica Lee, "Which Airlines and Cruise Lines Are Best Leveraging Facebook Pages?" *Inside Facebook*, July 16, 2009, available at http://www.insidefacebook.com/2009/07/16/which-airlines-and-cruise-lines-are-best-leveraging-facebook-pages/.

CHAPTER 10

1. Quoted in "National Leader of the Month for September 2007: Herb Kelleher," LeaderNetwork.org, September 2007, available at http://www.leadernetwork.org/herb_kelleher_september_07.htm.

2. Leigh Branham, *Keeping the People Who Keep You in Business: 24 Ways to Hang on to Your Most Valuable Talent* (New York: AMACOM, 2001), 55.

3. Joshua Freed, "Republic Wins Bid for Frontier, Beats Southwest," *Seattle Times*, August 13, 2009, available at http://seattletimes.nwsource.com/html/businesstechnology/2009652623_apusfrontiersouthwest.html.

4. Jody Hoffer Gittell, "Connecting with Employees through Front-Line Leadership: Lessons from Southwest Airlines," in *What Managers Say, What Employees Hear: Connecting with Your Front Line (So They'll Connect with Customers)*, edited by Regina Fazio Maruca (Westport, CT: Praeger, 2006), 125.

5. Gittell, "Connecting with Employees," 134–35.

6. Gittell, "Connecting with Employees," 135.

7. James L. Heskett and Leonard A. Schlesinger, "Leaders Who Shape and Keep Performance-Oriented Culture," in *The Leader of the Future*, edited by Frances Hesselbein, Marshall Goldsmith, and Richard Beckhard (San Francisco: Jossey-Bass, 1996), 115–16.

8. Heskett and Schlesinger, "Leaders Who Shape," 117.

9. Quoted in CPP Web site, "Southwest Airlines and the MBTI Assessment Creating a Corporate Culture That Soars: A Case Study of Southwest Airlines," 2006, 1, available at https://www.cpp.com/Pdfs/southwest_airlines_2006.pdf.

10. Quoted in CPP, "Southwest Airlines," 2.

11. Gary Kelly, "Gary's Corner: The Winning Spirit," *Spirit*, November 2008, available at http://www.spiritmag.com/2008_11/gary-kelly.php.

12. Charles Haanel, *The Master Key System* (Wilkes-Barre, PA: Kallisti Publishing, 2000).

13. Stephen R. Covey, *The 8th Habit: From Effectiveness to Greatness* (New York: Free Press, 2004), 317.

14. Covey, *8th Habit*, 317.

15. Dave Ridley, "Southwest Selects Wi-Fi for Our Fleet," *Nuts About Southwest*, August 21, 2009, available at http://www.blogsouthwest.com/blog/southwest-selects-wi-fi-our-fleet.

16. PRNewswire-FirstCall, "EPA Recognizes Southwest Airlines (Dallas & Houston Operations) for Leading Green Power Purchase," August 20, 2009, available at http://www.reuters.com/article/pressRelease/idUS190300+20-Aug-2009+PRN20090820.

17. PRNewswire-FirstCall, "EPA Recognizes Southwest Airlines (Dallas & Houston Operations) for Leading Green Power Purchase."

18. Lori Calabro, "It Must Be the Peanuts: Why Is Southwest, Alone among U.S. airlines, Healthy and Thinking about Growth Again?" *CFO*, December 1, 2001, available at http://www.cfo.com/article.cfm/3002388/c_3046495?f=insidecfo.

19. Calabro, "It Must Be the Peanuts."

20. Sara Minogue, "Southwest Airlines: America's Fourth Largest Airline Lets the Service Speak for Itself," *Boards*, October 1, 2002, available at http://www.boardsmag.com/articles/magazine/20021001/south.html.

21. Minogue, "Southwest Airlines."

22. Linda Loyd, "Southwest Airlines Posts $91M 1Q Loss," *Philadelphiu Inquirer*, April 16, 2009.

23. Loyd, "Southwest Airlines Posts $91 1Q Loss."

24. Dave Arnott, *Corporate Cults: The Insidious Lure of the All-Consuming Organization* (New York: AMACOM, 1999), 1.

Bibliography

The following are books that feature the story of Southwest Airlines and its leaders.

Cohan, Peter S. *Value Leadership: The 7 Principles That Drive Corporate Value in Any Economy.* San Francisco: Jossey-Bass, 2003.

Davidson, Paul. *Consumer Joe: Harassing Corporate America, One Letter at a Time.* New York: Broadway Books, 2003.

Doganis, Rigas. *The Airline Business in the 21st Century.* New York: Routledge, 2001.

Freiberg, Kevin, and Jackie Freiberg. *Nuts! Southwest Airlines' Crazy Recipe for Business and Personal Success.* New York: Broadway Books, 1998.

Gittell, Jody Hoffer. *The Southwest Airlines Way: Using the Power of Relationships to Achieve High Performance.* New York: McGraw-Hill, 2003.

Goddard, Larry, and David Brown. *The Turbo Charged Company: Igniting Your Business to Soar Ahead of the Competition.* York, UK: York Publishing Services, 1995.

Grubbs-West, Lorraine. *Lessons in Loyalty: How Southwest Airlines Does It—An Insider's View.* Dallas: CornerStone Leadership Institute, 2005.

Harris, Jim. *Getting Employees to Fall in Love with Your Company.* New York: AMACOM, 1996.

McConnell, Ben, and Jackie Huba. *Creating Customer Evangelists: How Loyal Customers Become a Volunteer Sales Force.* New York: Kaplan Business, 2007.

Muse, Lamar. *Southwest Passage: The Inside Story of Southwest Airlines' Formative Years.* Waco, TX: Eakin Press, 2003.

Newman, Winifred Barnum. *Gum Wrappers and Goggles.* Chicago: Summit, 1982.

Parker, James F. *Do the Right Thing: How Dedicated Employees Create Loyal Customers and Large Profits.* Upper Saddle River, NJ: Wharton School Publishing, 2007.

Pérezgonzález, Jose D. *Knowledge Management Edition Guide to Gittell's Book "The Southwest Airlines Way."* New Zealand: Jose D. Pérezgonzález, 2006.

Petzinger, Thomas Jr. *Hard Landing: The Epic Contest for Power and Profits That Plunged the Airlines into Chaos.* New York: Times Business/Random House, 1995.

Spector, Robert, and Fred Wiersema. *Customer Service: Extraordinary Results at Southwest Airlines, Charles Schwab, Lands' End, American Express, Staples, and USAA.* Darby, PA: Diane Publishing, 1998.

Thompson, Marty. *Flying for Peanuts: The ABCs of Flying Southwest Airlines.* Chandler, AZ: Five Star, 2003.

Whiteley, Richard, and Diane Hessan. *Customer-Centered Growth: Five Proven Strategies for Building Competitive Advantage.* New York: Basic Books, 1997.

Index

About the Author

CHRIS LAUER is the author of *Breaking Free: How to Quit Your Job and Start Your Own Business* (Praeger, 2009) and *The Management Gurus: Lessons from the Best Management Books of All Time* (Portfolio, 2008). He is a freelance writer and the editor-in-chief at Lauer Editorial Services, a company he started in 2006. Over the past decade, Lauer has written more than five hundred book reviews and book summaries for Soundview Executive Book Summaries. Many of his book reviews can be found on *BusinessWeek* Online. He can be contacted at delawareeditor@aol.com. Visit his Web site at www.laueredit.com.